M000285156

HEAD, HEART AND HARA

Head, Heart & Hara

The Soul Centres of
West and East

PETER WILBERG

New Gnosis Publications, London

First published by New Gnosis Publications
www.newgnosis.co.uk

© 2003 by Peter Wilberg
All rights reserved.

The right of Peter Wilberg to be identified as the author
of this work has been asserted by him in accordance
with the Copyright, Designs and Patents Act, 1988.

Printed and bound in England by Anthony Rowe Ltd
Distributed by Gardners Books, Eastbourne, Sussex

ISBN 1-904519-01-6

If you ask anyone where in his body he feels his 'I' he will probably consider it a strange question at first, but pressed for an answer, he will reply 'in the head' or 'in the chest' or he will indicate with a vague gesture the region of his stomach and heart. Only very rarely will anyone indicate a region further down....

Hara, the Vital Centre of Man

Karlfried Graf von Dürckheim

CONTENTS

PREFACE

As the Japanese philosopher Sato Tsuji pointed out:

It is the great error of Western philosophers that they always regard the human body intellectually, from the outside, as though it were not indissolubly a part of the active self.

A preface should tell us something about the matters with which a book deals. So let us begin, quite literally with the matter of this or any book – its materiality. Regarded "from the outside, intellectually" a book is a material body in space. It can also be understood as a vibrating energetic structure. The book's three-dimensional form, however, conceals a multi-dimensional inner world of *meaning*. We cannot enter this world by researching the fabric of space and time, matter and energy. We can only enter it by *reading* the book – letting our awareness flow into its inner soul-space – a space that derives from the unique soul qualities that constitute the spirit of another *being* – its author. The world of soul is a world of meaning. The world of spirit, a world of beings.

To convince a modern scientist of the existence of an invisible world of soul and spirit, however, is like trying to convince someone who doesn't know what it means to read, that the visible ink marks on the pages of a book conceal an *invisible world of meaning* and are the work of an *invisible being* – one nowhere to be found in the matter or energy of the book.

When early Greek and Chinese physicians sought to diagnose their patients' dis-ease, they did so through different forms of 'body-reading'. This included 'reading' their pulse or pulses. This did not mean simply sensing the quantitative regularity and strength of blood flows impelled by the heart, but sensing different subtle qualities of flow. For the traditional Oriental physician, these qualitative flows are flows, not of blood but of *qi*. Today, however, the terms *qi, ki* or *chi* are still thoughtlessly defined in the West as referring to a form of subtle 'energy'. The thoughtlessness lies firstly in ignoring the fact that the word *energy* itself is quintessentially Greek, and therefore has a sense and resonance that cannot be lightly equated with the meaning of a Chinese or Japanese character. *That* meaning is far closer to the Greek words *psyche* and *horme*, since qi refers both to a life-giving breath and to something which, like blood, hormones and emotions, also *flows*. The Greek word *horme*, like the words 'humours' and 'hormones', derives from the Sanskrit *sarmas* – a flowing. The physician's awareness of different qualities of flow was an attunement to the soul qualities and soul-body of the patient – to subtle qualities and flows of *awareness*.

Just as there are flows of air between and around bodies in space, so are there flows of awareness. There is a good reason therefore, why the word 'spirit' has its root in the Latin *spirare* – to breathe, and why the Greek word for spirit – *pneuma* – also meant air or wind. Just as we breathe air into the physical spaces of our bodies, so do we also breathe in our *awareness* of the world around us. So too, in breathing out, do we give expression to that awareness as *speech*. The Greek word *psyche* means the vitalising breath of awareness we take into and release from our souls as speech (*logos*).

The modern term 'psychology' derives from the Greek words *psyche* (soul or life-breath) and *logos* (word or speech). Its most literal meaning is 'the speech of the soul'. It was Heraclitus (circa 500 BC) who first conjoined the words *psyche* and *logos* in a single saying, one that itself speaks from the depths of the soul, which still stands today as the founding and grounding principle of any true 'psychology': "You will not find any bounds to the *psyche* by going about its surface, even if you explore every single direction, so deep is its *logos*."

Here the message of the Greek sage is identical to that of the Chinese sage *Lao Tse*. Heraclitus tells us that the speech of the psyche is eternal and unfathomable, something that "men fail to comprehend both before hearing it and after they have heard." Lao Tse tells us that "The way (*Dao*) that can be spoken is not the eternal way." But the Chinese character for *Dao* also means 'to say'. Lao Tse's famous opening saying can therefore be read in the following way, "The saying that is spoken is not the true saying." Why? Because meaning or sense is never something that can be represented in words but is what communicates silently through the word (*dialogos*). The inner sense of a word is not simply its reference to some 'thing' we are aware of but its inner resonance – the way it gives expression to subtle tones and shades *of* awareness as such.

The material outwardness of the human body, like that of a book, is also a language. Its true inwardness does not consist of flows of 'subtle energy' – the axiom of New Age 'energy medicine'. Instead, the subtle 'energy' known as *chi, ki* or *qi* is, in essence, a flow of subtle meanings or senses shaped by a subtle language of the soul – its *logos* or *Dao*. This language gives expression to subtle qualities of awareness in our inner soul-space of awareness. It also gives shape to an inner *body of awareness* – our soul-body. The inner soul-space of this body includes more than the inner mind space of our head and the inner emotional spaces of our chest and *heart*. Its true centre is not an 'energy centre' but a *centre of awareness* in our belly and lower abdomen – that *abode* of the soul known in Japanese as *hara*.

Western culture is a culture of *head* and *heart*. Eastern culture acknowledges that deeper centre of awareness in the belly known as *hara*. *Head, heart and hara* however, are not 'energy centres' but *soul centres* – centres of awareness within a singular soul-spiritual *body of awareness*. For, as the masters of Daoist 'internal alchemy' recognised, awareness is not a vacuum or void waiting to be filled with sensations stemming from the material world. That is because, like meaning or sense, awareness possesses its own immaterial reality, it has its own immanent *sensual* qualities that are intrinsically meaningful – these being elemental *soul* qualities of warmth and coolness, light and darkness, fluidity and solidity, each with their own *spiritual* substantiality.

When we truly experience the human body from the inside, instead of regarding it "intellectually, from the outside", what we experience is the *fleshly shape and substantiality* of our inner *body* of awareness – our body of soul and spirit. The recognition, rediscovery and 'resurrection' of this body – the *soma-psychikos* or *soma-peumatikos* of the New Testament, the *Dharma body* of Buddhism and the *golden embryo* of Daoist tradition – constitutes the *unifying* wisdom of West and East. This is the wisdom I call *soma-psychology* and *soma-spirituality,* the key to which is *hara awareness.*

It is not the wisdom traditions of the East alone that have guarded the flame of spiritual truth. It was kept alive and glowing in the sayings of Heraclitus. It was rekindled in the thinking of the twentieth-century German philosopher Martin Heidegger when he wrote of man's *dis-location* from the true centre and deep inner ground of his being. 'Dis-location' is the literal meaning of the German word for madness – 'Ver-rücktheit'. But to see madness as 'mental' illness is itself testament to the madness of modern psychology and psychiatry. For, a truly scientific psychology would recognise that so-called 'mental' illness is, in essence, a disturbance in the individual's relation to their own inwardly sensed body and inner bodily sense of self. The generalised pathology of individuals in Western culture is an exclusive identification with their own head and upper body awareness – resulting in an incapacity to *ground* their self-awareness in their lower body, and *centre* it in the hara.

The paradigm of our globalised Western culture understands life as an *outward* movement of awareness from self to world. An earlier Indian paradigm understood life as an inward movement of awareness from *world to self*. A third, Oriental paradigm understood life as a balance or rhythm of outward and inward movements. This book introduces a fourth paradigm – not an outward but an *inward* movement of awareness from *self to world*. For, the inward movement of awareness from self to world is a way that can lead us, through hara awareness, to a deeper sense of *inner connectedness* to the world – connecting our own innermost being with that of others.

Karlfried Graf von Dürckheim, author of the classic work 'Hara, the Vital Centre of Man', was the first European thinker to acknowledge the soma-spiritual profundity of *hara awareness*, and to propound and promote it in the West. His words also convey the way of the *fourth paradigm*.

Man's way inward is the way of uniting himself with his Being, wherein he partakes of life beyond space and time...To realise Being in all and everything then becomes the sole function of his life.

HEAD, HEART AND HARA
The Soul Centres of West and East

Introduction

We speak with our physical bodies. We listen with our souls. The 'listening soul' is the body as we experience it psychically, from within. It houses mental, emotional and spiritual 'regions' or 'spaces', each with its own centre. Head, Heart and Hara is about the spiritual physiology of the three principal centres of this body-soul. The word 'physio-logy' derives from the Greek verbs *phuein* – to cultivate or engender, and *legein* – to gather and lay out. What is gathered and laid out in words must first be wordlessly cultivated and engendered in our listening. From each of the three soul-centres we listen in a different way, make a different sort of inner contact with ourselves and each other, and therefore also speak with a different voice.

The evolution of human thinking, values and religion has a great deal to do with the relation between these three centres, the relative value attached to them, and the type of thinking that corresponds to each of them. Scientific thinking is head thinking. Christianity emphasises the heart. Judaism and Islam are based on prophetic speech – the vocal and linguistic imagination that arises between head and heart. Buddhism focuses on the 'soul-belly' or 'hara' – the seat of intuition, will and intent. The contact we make with each other from the hara is neither intellectual nor emotional but 'umbilical', extending from an energy point a few inches below the navel.

1

For most people, such direct umbilical soul-contact is something they expect only in intimate relationships or through finding a 'soul-mate'. Otherwise, human connectedness at this level is experienced only indirectly through the sense of 'we-ness' brought about by friendships, close relationships, family and community.

The figure of the human soul-body can be pictured as three spheres, one on top of the other, whose size varies from one individual to another. Lacking the experience of umbilical contact from the hara, people walk about like top-heavy lollipops, able to make contact with one another only from the upper two spheres of head and heart. They may sense the mysterious lower sphere, the soul-sphere of the belly or hara. They may long for relationships and communication that touch the depths of soul that are harboured there. But they are unable to actively make a connection with others *from* these soul-depths. Instead, they wait for this to 'happen' through a relationship – without any activity on their part – or pursue it through head and heart communication alone, hoping that this might somehow bring them into contact with themselves and others at a soul level. What they do not realise is that no amount of verbal or physical contact with others will bring this about. For, the level of soul-contact we achieve with others is not a question of what people talk about or how intimate we are with each other – verbally or physically – but about how we listen.

Contact from the hara is an inner listening contact, one that is available to us at any time, whether with friend or colleague, lover or stranger, simply by cultivating our ability to bear with others in pregnant silence. But if conversation means nothing more than taking it in turns to speak, without any depth of inner listening contact with others, then, however intimate the subject, there will be no real soul-contact. Only by learning to be with others in silence, not just while they speak but in the intervals of silence that precede and follow their words, do we learn to open our hara – the 'soul-womb' of our listening.

Some therapists and counsellors, for example, listen from this place – their soul-wombs are open and receptive and they choose to be therapists precisely in order to allow themselves this openness. And yet, they are able to respond to their clients only from the head or the heart. They have not yet experienced what it means to actively communicate from the hara – from the still-point of silence within themselves.

Not just when we offer counsel or care to others but whenever we listen to another person speak we have an opportunity to make umbilical contact from the hara. But an education that values only powers of speech, reasoning and verbal articulation does not teach people how to listen, nor brings them closer to the wordless inner knowing that is seated in the hara. It is not by speaking but only by withholding the spoken word that we give time for embryonic intuitions to germinate and gestate in this womb of souls; only by holding to the still-point of silence within ourselves can we 'be-hold' the inner meaning of someone's words in our listening imagination.

Hara is a word rooted in Japanese and Zen-Buddhist culture. Amongst the countries of Europe it is principally the German language and culture, with its embedded notions of *innerlichkeit* (inwardness), *gemüt* (soul-warmth) and *geborgenheit* (inner security), that also preserves a sense of the human 'soul-belly' or 'soul-womb' – the hara. For example, the German concept of 'gründlichkeit' – normally read as 'thoroughness' or 'German efficiency' – translates literally as 'groundedness'. It corresponds to the Japanese notion of *haragei* – any activity or art-form finely tuned with hara. In both countries this traditionally included fighting and war. But the basis of war is not the soul-womb or hara, on the contrary it is the isolation, splitting off and repression of man's spiritual centre whether this takes place within the individual, the family – or within the global family of nations.

For people in the West it is a spiritual challenge to ground their speaking and listening, thinking and feeling, in the essence of their own being – to lower their centre of consciousness to the hara. For the Japanese, the challenge of Western culture has been the converse – to freely allow feelings and creative thinking to rise from the hara to the personality centres of heart and head without losing their depth of character and spiritual groundedness. But the global technological culture that meanwhile has come to dominate the world, ruled by the thinking of the head, now threatens to swamp the last traces of both European and Japanese spirituality, and with it, the understanding of the soul-womb or soul-belly. Christian spirituality tends to be reduced to elevated spiritual feeling (centred in the heart), posturing moral fundamentalism (centred in the head), or evangelism – preaching rather than listening. After the violent and explosive excesses of the Crusades, when Christianity literally spilled its guts and those of its foes, it began to lose its guts – to lose its hara. In Japan, head thinking is undermining the 'thinking of the belly' and replacing hara with sex comics, Western emotionality and 'Christian' heart values. This is partly a consequence of Buddhism's earlier, almost exclusive concentration on man's inner being, centred in the hara. And yet Buddhism also inherited from Indian religious culture a knowledge of the *multiple* centres or 'chakras' of the human soul-body. This 'Old Age' wisdom is passed on unchanged by followers of 'New Age' philosophies as if there had been no historic change or movement in the spiritual 'centre' or 'assemblage point' of man's being since the time of the Rishis. Nor has there been any attempt to explore the contemporary relevance of this historical evolution for the 'New Age' millennium. To do so means forging an evolutionary philosophy, psychology and physiology of the soul-body, one based on the essential truths of Western and Eastern spiritual traditions – on head, heart *and* hara.

Head, Heart and Hara is a prophetic work in the Jewish tradition, pointing to a new spiritual centre in the making, a new evolutionary 'assemblage point' of human consciousness. I believe that this millennium will see a major shift in the nature of human thinking – from today's purely verbal-intellectual thinking, a 'thinking in words' – to a type of wordless intellectual intuition rooted in inward listening. The speech centre of human consciousness, sited between head and heart, will be relinked to the centre of our wordless listening – the hara. This will generate a new centre of consciousness between heart and hara. Whereas the speech centre between head and heart is the centre of our *linguistic imagination*, this new centre is the focal point of our *listening imagination*. The social evolution of this centre was aborted by the Holocaust and the Second World War, and is now obstructed by the illusory images of our global technological, media and drug culture.

The difference between the wordless listening imagination and our verbal linguistic imagination can be compared to the difference between radio, on the one hand, and television or computers on the other. The 'images' of the listening imagination do not have a merely representational, iconic or symbolic function, like those of the visual media. They are not pictures framed by a screen or 'visualised' in the head, but subtle impressions of the soul; impressions which do not represent words or texts but arise from our wordless intuition and float on the fluid surface of our feelings. The thinking that arises from the listening imagination is a fluid thinking, one which gives time for nascent intuitions to surface from the soul-womb of our listening and take shape as soul-impressions – as listening 'in-sights'. These insights express the inner rationality of the soul – a rationality far deeper than that of the linguistic imagination. Knowledge based on speech, language and linguistic imagination is always a *translation* of a more fundamental type of knowing – a wordless inner knowing rooted in the hara. Yet, both religion and the sciences identify knowledge not with this wordless inner knowing but with its representation in words and images. By contrast, the poet is a true 'fundamentalist', aware that all language is a *translation* of essentially wordless comprehensions. That is why true poetry is an exercise, not just of the linguistic imagination and verbal artistry but of the intuitive, listening imagination. The listening imagination is the basis, not only of poetry but of musical composition, of waking-life insights and of our capacity to recall our nightly dreams. Through it, we can transform our listening into a type of lucid waking dream ('clairvoyance'), into a type of lucid inner hearing ('clairaudience') and into a type of silent inner knowing or 'channelling'.

.

The Thinking of the Head and Heart

Ask any Westerner where his thinking is centred and he will point to his head. It appears self-evident to him that we think with our heads and that our brains are the physical organ of the intellect. Someone who thinks poorly doesn't have his head 'screwed on'. Someone clever is 'brainy'. The truth in this view of the mind is that the thinking of the head does indeed run on fixed 'neuro-linguistic' tracks. Words are the stations on these neurological rail tracks of the mind. Language is the network of thought-lines that connects them. People live their mental lives in different local areas of this network, their thinking shuttling automatically between the word-stations on each line, or making standard crossovers to other lines.

Some people, for example, live in an area called the Business Network. Here there is a large central station called Free Market (formerly 'Mammon'). Off it run a whole host of lines such as the Management Line, the Technology Line etc. The 'real world' of the people who inhabit this network is defined by its language – it is the 'global market' for labour and commodities. Other words in this language include *user, system, stock, resource, market, customer, skill and productivity.* Through them, the thinking of the head reduces the earth to a (declining) stock of exploitable mineral 'reserves', plants and animals to 'gene-stocks', and human beings to a reservoir of exploitable skills and knowledge – to Human Resources.

Other people live close to the Spiritual Network. Here there is a large central station, known as 'God', from which run lines such as Jesus, Allah, Buddha, Shiva and Vishnu. If, for some reason, you miss the connection to God you can always get an inter-city to Science or Free Market. Alternatively you might buy a ticket to New Age, Therapy or Mind and Body. Here the number of lines gets quite confusing. The Unconscious, Transference and Projection are all on the main line to Psychoanalysis. Vitamins, Exercise and Positive Thinking are popular stations on the Health and Vitality line. Ordinary commuter lines on Network Up and Down include a whole number of stations such as Feel-good, High Spirits, Low and Down, Their Fault, Resentment and 'Whose Line is it Anyway'? The point about the countless networks of the Language Mind is that the thinking that takes place through them admits of no real questioning.

The point about the countless networks of the Language Mind is that the thinking that takes place through them admits of no real questioning. Like the Jehovah's Witness at your door, they provide an automatic answer to every question. One has only to call up another quotation from the Bible, invoke a sacred word like 'global competitiveness' or 'medical evidence', utter a dark mantra like 'evil' or 'unconscious resistance', or, as a last resort, go back to the central stations of Faith, Science, Ethics and Reason.

Immunity to fundamental questioning characterises the 'scientific' mind as much as the religious, commercial or psychoanalytic mind. Serious scientific 'minds' earnestly debate whether 'intelligence' is 'determined' by our genes or by our upbringing and environment, as if there was absolutely no question about the meaning of the word 'intelligence'. Rarely do they question why what we call intelligence should be reduced to whatever it is that IQ tests test. For to do so would mean temporarily suspending the thinking of the head with its stock lexicon of mutually defining terms. Eventually, serious questions do break through, however. Someone bright intuits that there may be many 'types' of intelligence, some of them connected perhaps with feeling. No sooner have they found scientific-sounding terms for these, however, than these terms themselves become unquestioned concepts. Suddenly, terms like 'emotional intelligence' become stock phrases and whole books are written on them. Such writing appeals because it appears to offer something that questions and transcends the thinking of the head. But the fact that we need to create special categories of 'spatial', 'verbal' or 'emotional intelligence' merely confirms the fact that we have not yet questioned what 'intelligence' as such – or thinking itself – really is. Both traditional and new concepts of intelligence, therefore, are basically an old one – the thinking of the head. To think in a genuinely new way about intelligence it is not enough to write intelligibly or intelligently. To write about other types of intelligence the writer must first be prepared to suspend the type of intelligence that they ordinarily apply in their writing. To explore other types of thinking we must first be prepared to suspend the thinking of the head, and to see the role that unquestioned terminology and phraseology plays in it.

Wording is worlding: the words we use to think about the world and to label our own perceptions and feelings actually shape that world – moulding our perceptions and feelings in their image. We dwell within our world as we dwell within the words we habitually use to think about it – either in a questioning or unquestioning way.

But to really question is to suspend the thinking of the head, and instead to *listen* to ourselves in a deeper way. Only then do we begin to hear the automatic assumptions and verbal rail tracks on which our head thinking runs. Suspending this head thinking means letting ourselves leave the mental word stations of the mind and take a walk in the natural landscape of our feelings and our *felt sense* of meaning. Western religious culture, Christianity in particular, does have a dim sense of another kind of thinking – one that rests in the heart and in feeling rather than in the head and intellect. It is a contemplative rather than calculative thinking, connected, like the word 'thinking' itself with 'thanking'. The thinking of the heart is a thoughtfulness which is rooted in a basic feeling of thankfulness for all that is. It is a thinking which thankfully gathers and lays out the harvest of experience. This gathering and laying out was the original meaning of the Greek verb *legein* ('to speak') and is the forgotten root of the word 'logic' itself.

The connection between thinking, speaking and 'gathering' is echoed in the English phrase 'I gather...', which does not imply a result of a logical analysis but suggests instead a sort of implicit or wordless understanding. The idea of 'gathering' is also echoed in the German verb *lesen* ('to read') which meant originally 'to glean'. The thinking of the heart is also a type of 'gleaning' or 'reading' – as when we use instinctive feeling to 'read' someone's body language, or, when as in earlier cultures, people were able to instinctively 'read' nature itself with their feelings. It was this type of instinctive reading that turned later into a reading of 'signs' — at first the stars and what was 'written' in them, and then the written word itself. Astrology, though ironically regarded by many as superstitious nonsense today, marked the transition from a thinking of the heart to the thinking of the head. It was indeed a precursor of modern science, not because it involved mathematical calculation but because 'head thinking' is above all *representational* thinking.

It was through astrology that man began to consistently *re*-present in signs and symbols what he felt, feared in his heart, or hoped was 'presencing' itself or 'coming to presence'. The canopy of the stars was experienced as a sort of arching cosmic skullcap, one which placed the human head – itself rounded like a planet, at its centre. This was not a thought but a specific experience of earlier times. Men's heads were literally open to the stars, and through the thinking of the head, mankind felt itself to be at the centre of a divine language, a language which seemed to overarch or surround the head in the same way that the stars seemed to overarch or surround the planet.

Today, few people consciously experience their verbal thoughts in this way, as tangible entities. Nevertheless, when someone explains an event in their life by saying 'that's my Moon in Aries' they are ritually invoking astrological language for the same reason that the priests of the past ritually invoked the gods of the heavens. By translating a feeling understanding of their experience into astrospeak they can hallow and sanctify it with astrological language ie. with the sacred terms of their own head thinking. Lest we should laugh at this, it is important to point out that astrologically-minded people are not alone in this. Whenever we call upon particular words and terminologies to make sense of our feelings and of events that affect us we are doing the same. The fact that we do so less consciously and self-consciously than an astrologer is nothing to boast of. The staunchest advocates of 'rational scientific' world outlook constantly employ physical metaphors and symbols in no less blatant, but certainly less *conscious* ways than astrologers do. The latter use the sun and planets as metaphors of feelings and states of being. Scientists talk of evidence 'standing up', of 'demolishing' a theory, of 'pursuing' truth or of quantum 'fields' or quantum 'leaps'.

Metaphorical representation using words and verbal imagery is an intrinsic and unavoidable part of language and of 'reasoning' itself. It is the essence of head thinking, which inhabits a world, not of star signs, but of linguistic signs – the world of words and word images.

Today, these are in evidence everywhere, not just in books or newspapers but on advertising posters, on televisions, computers and all modern multi-media. In fact, not only words and images but society's cultural and manufacturing products, however solid and material, are nowadays signs. Marx pointed out that the capitalist world is an accumulation of commodities. The monetary value of these commodities, however, is now very much connected not only with their use-value but with their symbolic value – with what they re-present. It is this symbolic value that allows advertisers to use the thinking of the head to appeal to the heart. Not only words and images, but products and services themselves, are all designed to give us an inner *feeling* of value – but only in order that we should then identify the inner value with a symbolic one, the inner feeling with its outer fetish – the commodity. The aim is to get us to 'fetishise' or worship the commodity by turning it into an idol of a sought after feeling or value, one whose brand name or corporate logo will become for us a religious icon.

The thinking of the head corresponds to the modern Western concept of 'mind'. In early Greek culture, however, the modern concept of mind had not developed, nor was there any word which referred to the living human body as a whole. The soul was experienced as an animating power in the chest – the *thumos*. Both physical strength and soul-strength were connected not with 'body' or 'mind' but with what today we would call 'having heart'. Thinking was not experienced as a process of conceptualisation going on in the head but as a hearing of voices. In intense emotional situations these voices were often projected outwards and experienced as those of the gods. Thus the heroes described by Homer did not think – they heard. They did not come to independent 'rational' decisions. They were impelled by the voices of the gods. This was a culture based on *mythos*. It was only through the Greek concept of the *logos* that mythic culture eventually gave way to what we call 'rational' thinking. This was based on the idea of a universal inner order within the cosmos – an impersonal 'logic' that human speech and human thinking could reflect. The Greek word *logos* can be variously translated as 'word', 'speech', 'account' or 'report'. The sayings of Heraclitus, however, show that originally this *logos* was not identified with the accounts of the truth represented in language and speech but with the inner speech of the *psyche*.

Again, it was Heraclitus who first conjoined the words *psyche* and *logos* in a saying which, historically, constitutes the founding statement of 'psychology'.

> You will not find any bounds to the *psyche*
> by going about its surface,
> even if you explore every single direction -
> so deep is its inner *logos*.

The *logos* he referred to was not ordinary speech but something more like 'soul-sense' – the inner resonance or reverberation of the *psyche*. That is why he could say that 'although this *logos* is ever-present, men fail to comprehend it, both before hearing it and once they have heard.' We hear the soul speak in the silences which precede, follow and accompany speech. We hear it speak also in language – by listening to the hidden *logos* or soul-sense of words themselves.

It was in the evolution of Hellenic and Hebrew culture that verbal meaning and felt sense, head thinking and heart thinking began to be separated. At the same time they remained strongly bound by the speech centre between head and heart – for this encompassed both poetic, rhetorical and reasoning powers. It was only in the Roman era that the human head and its thinking began to dominate speech, and dominate the heart, using both reason and rhetoric to serve the calculative political purposes of the ego, the newly-crowned 'emperor' of the human soul. Stoic philosophers fought a rearguard battle for truth, preparing the way for a Christianity which sought to rebalance head and heart – to affirm the universality, not of reason alone but of love and compassion.

Both Judaism and Islam were religions based on prophetic thinking. This is a thinking that has its source not in the head or heart alone but in speech. The human speech centre is the source of prophetic, vocal inspiration. Just as the Greeks had heard the gods speak, so did the prophets hear the word of God or of his angels. But in Judaism the worship of God as a divine 'Thou' whom one addresses or is addressed by in speech went hand in hand with a parallel elevation of the linguistic ego or 'I'. Like God, the word 'I' is universal, impersonal and featureless, whatever language it is spoken in. Thus whenever we say 'I did this' or 'I saw that' or 'I felt this' we imply an unchangeable self that is not touched or altered by what it does, feels, hears or sees. The divinisation of the linguistic 'I' through its equally featureless mirror image or counterpart – the divine 'Thou' – provided a stable ego-centre for the thinking of the head, one by which it could finally separate itself from the human body and human heart, overseeing it like a satellite or moon which orbits the earth. By contrast, Christianity sought initially to once again centre man's being in the heart, to establish the Kingdom of Heaven on earth, and in the human body and heart – as the word become flesh.

Today science still locates conscious awareness 'within' the brain, as if the brain and everything else that we can study were not itself a phenomenon within our conscious awareness. Science also seeks to maintain a 'thinking of the head'. Indeed through technology it even seeks to externalise its basic principle – binary thinking – in computer and electronic information networks. Ordinary everyday thinking also remains stubbornly rooted in the dualistic mental concepts of 'intellect' and 'emotion' which mirror an underlying division of head and heart. Thus the conflict between reason and emotion, mind and body, commercialism and spirituality, calculation and compassion continues unabated.

The Thinking of the Belly

Western culture is essentially a 'head and heart' culture, with Christianity emphasising the heart, and science the head. Many seemingly 'emotional' people actually 'feel with their heads'. Instead of listening to themselves they acknowledge only feelings they can immediately label with mental or spoken words, and use these to avoid other, less tangible feelings. Paradoxically, it is these very words that may then trigger or intensify their emotions. Many apparently sober and unemotional people, on the other hand, actually 'think with their hearts'. Their verbal reasoning is both a rationalisation of their feelings and a protection against other feelings they do not wish to face. A truly 'objective' thinking is one that is prepared to see and bear the truth. This can only arise if we are conscious of the interplay of head and heart, conscious of our language and the way we use it. This means being conscious of our thoughts before we speak them. It also means being conscious of all our feelings – and prepared to really feel them – before we label or rationalise them. Such an understanding of our own heads and hearts can only arise from a place in ourselves that under-stands them. This is the belly or hara in Japanese – the true centre of gravity of both body and soul. As Karlfried Graf von Dürckheim explained in 'Hara, the Vital Centre of Man':

> Hara de kangaeru (to think with the belly) is the opposite of atama de kangaeru (to think with the head)...The Japanese says, tapping his forehead with his finger 'Koko de kangaeru no wa ikemasen.', 'One must not think just with this.', and often adds, 'Hara de kangaenasai.', 'Please think with your belly.' By this he means, 'not so rationally, intellectually, but deeper please, as a whole person from the essence of your being.'

Hara means 'belly' in Japanese, but it refers not to the physical stomach but to something more like our capacity 'to stomach' things – to digest experience, absorb meaning from it and respond to events from a place of inner strength and composure. Having hara is equivalent in *everyday* speech to what in slang English is called having 'guts' or 'bottle'. In Western culture this is usually identified with machismo and military 'erectness'. Physical power is not seen as centred in the belly as it is in Sumo, but is instead identified with a manly chest and a powerful head for butting with. That is why Western man, like the Western cartoon 'superhero' with his big head and inflated chest, is seen as top-heavy and unbalanced in the East. In Japan the Western superhero is judged as having no guts. In Eastern culture having 'guts' is expressed through inner composure and a physical posture with its centre of gravity in the belly.

We all have 'gut feelings' and 'gut instincts'. But we each need to learn how to *think* as well as feel from our bellies – how to listen to our intuitions and express them, listen to our impulses and follow them. This is not 'irrationalism', for it is only by listening to, trusting and following the thinking of the belly that we discover the inner rationality of these intuitions and impulses – one which transcends the thinking of the head and heart. In the West, expressions such as 'feeling gutted' or 'hitting below the belt' give a crude and somewhat negative connotation to the guts. Western culture has demonised the regions 'below the belt', seeing them as an instinctual 'underworld' of aggression and sexual drives. This results in the splitting off and repression of man's physical and spiritual centre of gravity – the hara. It is this spiritual repression that fosters rage, violence and sexual obsession, not to mention the endless psychological tangles and tensions between head and heart, which are cut off from their source and ground in the hara.

The thinking of the head and heart results, paradoxically, in alternating cycles of cold reason and emotional heat, compassion and heartlessness, mindfulness and mindlessness. Hara, on the other hand, is related to the Zen practice of *mushin*, a term which means 'no heart, no mind'. *Mushin* is not what we in the West would call a 'whole-hearted' attention to something but a single-pointed concentration on 'no-thing' – on the still-point of silence in the hara. To contact our essential inner being through the hara means practicing *mushin* – emptying our hearts and heads and clearing an empty space in our souls – not in order to achieve ego-lessness, non-being or 'nirvana' but in order to allow genuinely new impulses and intuitions to enter our souls and germinate within us.

The Japanese word *mu* from which *mushin* is derived, means 'no' or 'no-thing'. It is also a mantra of Zen Buddhism, referred to in many koans. These are paradoxical questions posed by the Zen masters in order to shift the student's centre of consciousness to a place beyond intellect and feeling – a place of 'no heart' and 'no mind'. 'Mu' is also the Greek root of the words 'mystic', 'mystical' and 'mysticism'. The *mustai* were the mute initiates or 'closed-mouthed ones' – those who bore the Mysteries within them in silence, and who opened their souls to receive the inner word or *logos*. In the Western spiritual tradition we can find an equivalent to *mushin* in the sayings of the Greek sage and initiate Heraclitus. We also hear it echoed in the philosophy of the medieval German mystic Meister Eckhart.

I once had a dream. I dreamt that I, even though a man, was pregnant, pregnant and full with Nothingness like a woman who is with child. And that out of this Nothingness, God was born.

Eckhart spoke of the soul as the virgin 'womb' and fruitful 'wife' of the spirit. He also spoke of a 'ghostly spot' in the soul which is 'matter-free' and which links us to our spiritual essence. The belly or hara is the site of this receptive and fertile 'soul-womb'.

In Buddhism the belly has always been understood as the centre and inner ground of man's being. The lack of visible exterior signs of 'progress' in many traditional Buddhist cultures is a reflection of a value system in which interest in the products of the head and the processes of the heart were subordinated to a concentration on man's inner being. Western materialism is based on the values of Doing and Having, of achievement and ful-filment – filling the belly, answering the mind's questions and filling it with knowledge, satisfying the heart's desires. And yet it is precisely this materialism that can leave people feeling empty rather than fulfilled. Western philosophy is in essence the philosophy of Being, eastern philosophy is a philosophy of Emptiness.

Western man identifies Being with intellectual and emotional creativity and fulfilment, but despite the fullness of head and heart, the physical stomach feels drained and spiritually empty – for he lacks hara. Eastern man identifies Being with emptiness of head and heart – only to explode with the energy compressed in the hara. Yet there is an essential truth in the Buddhist practice of emptying, one which is in perfect accord with the creative impulse of the West, and has nothing to do with the attainment of a state of pure emptiness or Nirvana. This is the understanding that it is only if we are able to actively clear an empty space in our head, heart and hara – our thoughts, feelings, impulses and intuitions – do we become open ourselves to receive genuinely new thoughts, sense genuinely new feelings, and let genuinely new intuitions and impulses germinate and incubate within us. This was Meister Eckhart's understanding of the virgin conception. The purpose of creating a 'virgin' soul is to become permanently fruitful in soul, and in this way to become host to a new sense of self – one linked to Being or 'God'. For God is essentially 'bearing'. Eckhart's thinking was a 'thinking of the belly', understood in a fundamentally feminine way through Christian symbolism – as the pregnant 'soul-womb' of the spirit.

Westerners tend to be embarrassed by 'pregnant' pauses of silence in conversation, experiencing them as a break in contact. Even today, however, the Westerner will note to some extent the Japanese capacity, not just for tolerating intervals of silence, but for experiencing within them a type of inner listening contact and communication with others. This type of silent intercourse or 'belly talk' has a special, intimate quality, but one that is dependent neither on the verbal exchange of ideas and feelings nor on touch and physical intimacy. It emanates from deep within the hara – the 'belly' or 'womb' of our listening. It is a type of 'umbilical' contact rather than one established from the head or heart.

The myth of Western culture is that we make contact with ourselves and other human beings through thinking, feeling or verbal communication. In fact we only ever make contact with another human being by listening inwardly to ourselves and getting in touch with the part of ourselves that is already in contact with them. Inward listening is not merely 'introspection', or a way of getting in touch with ourselves. It is the basis of our inner listening contact and communication with others. Body language may express this inner listening communication but the true basis of 'non-verbal communication' is not the speaking body but the listening soul. Our inner listening connectedness with others is a direct soul-to-soul communication – not an expression of the soul via the body. It is also a form of inner support that we grant to others. This is its therapeutic value. The Indo-European root of the word 'therapy' is *dher* – to bear or support. A bridge must be able to stand the strain and support the weight of what crosses it. So too our listening. But 'to bear' is not just to withstand. It is also to carry and bring to ripeness something that is pregnant within us. To truly 'bear with' someone as they speak is therefore not just to listen patiently, compassionately or supportively. It is quite literally to *bear* with them and bear *with* them, to be open to receive that which they find unbearable, or difficult to bear, into the womb of one's own soul – to tend it and help bring it to fruition.

Sometimes, when we listen, it can feel as if a space in our heads is filling to bursting point with thoughts, or our hearts with emotion. But the more deeply and meditatively we listen the more an inner time-space expands within us. This space is felt lower down, in the region of the belly – rather like a psychic womb. It is akin to the type of time-space experienced by the foetus – a spacious present that is not yet divided into past, present and future. The 'listening body' that houses this time-space is not the belly or womb per se, but the body *as* a womb – the womb whose waters are the fluid medium of *feeling tone*.

Feeling tones are not emotions like those we experience in our hearts and breasts and express in our vocal tones. They are the inner tones or chords of our being on which all thoughts and feelings ride. In the same way that the foetus rests in the waters of the womb, it is in these tones of silence that our listening self rests and floats. They are its fluid medium and buoyant ground. Subtle, dreamlike inner impressions and images surface from feeling tones surrounding the listening self. These are impressions and images that we can only fully 'be-hold' by looking inwardly and 'holding' them in our inner gaze. The art of meditative listening is founded on our capacity to be and 'bear with' others in pregnant silence, to hearken from the still-point of silence within the soul-womb of our bellies and give time for these inner impressions to gather and gestate within us in a dreamlike way. In this way we transform our listening into a type of inner seeing or clairvoyance – the 'in-sight' of the *listening imagination.*

Between head and heart is the seat of vocal inspiration and the linguistic imagination. Between heart and hara is the seat of our non-verbal, listening imagination. This operates at a level of consciousness beneath our conscious waking thoughts. Only by giving ourselves time to be with others in silence without responding in speech – by restraining the speech centre between head and heart – can we begin to awaken this listening imagination. First, however, we need to hearken, alone, to the still-point of silence within ourselves – to our 'foetal' or listening self. This is rather like dropping anchor within ourselves, sinking into the soul-womb of our bellies and extending an umbilical cord into its centre. As we do so we experience an inward expansion of the 'soul-space' within us – the listening body – which can enlarge from the hara to embrace head and heart and extend even beyond the physical body itself. Within it we can receive and bear the inner being of the other person in the larger 'soul-womb' of our listening.

Like the foetus in the womb, the inner being of an individual – the listening self – is not something outwardly visible or audible. Nor is the inner listening contact we establish with another human being a physical contact. Only if our souls are fertile, if we let ourselves be inwardly penetrated and impregnated by another person's words, does something then grow within that allows us to forge and

16

maintain this inner contact. It is as if we bear the other person's 'soul-child' within us, and are in contact with them through it. It is this soul-child of the other that we bring to fruition and bear back to the other in our listening. Our listening body is its mother or womb. Our listening self – our foetal self – shares this womb with it, and is connected with it somewhat like two babies who are linked umbilically by a common cord.

Very few people are able to make this umbilical contact with others directly from their spiritual centre. And yet it is the hidden basis of all communication. We cannot make true inner contact with another human being in any outward way, whether through words or through physical touch. We can do so only by first getting in touch with the part of ourselves that *is* in contact with them, that is on their 'wavelength'. This means reaching down to the still-point of silence in the hara, and getting in touch with others from it. This reaching down and into ourselves is the true meaning of 'in-tending'.

The hara is a centre not of thinking or feeling but of will or intent. To make contact with someone from the hara is to communicate from the will – to touch them with our 'in-tending'. Buddhist physiology has long acknowledged a point a few inches below the navel called the 'tanden', where we can feel the energy of our will physically, sense the umbilical 'tendril of intent' that can reach out to touch others from the womb of our listening. The hara is the spiritual centre of 'true will', because within it we can clear a receptive and fertile space that is not filled with preconceived urges, desires, or plans, but can 'will' because it allows itself to 'want' or 'lack'. Fasting and ascetic practices that empty the belly of food or deprive the body of physical pleasures confuse creating this clear space within the 'soul-belly' or hara with having an empty stomach, or with deliberately intensifying unfulfilled needs.

The hara is also the source of our intuition. It is the clear space within the 'soul-belly' that turns it into the intuitive 'womb' of our listening. Within it, we are literally open to receive the word of others without 'pre-conception' – and bring it to fruition within ourselves. The 'tendril of intent' is the spiritual umbilicus that we extend from the *tanden* below the navel to the inner being – the listening self – that lurks within the belly of the other. Listening from the hara we touch the other person with our listening body, our listening intent and intuition. Their conscious speaking personality may not be immediately conscious of this touch, but the inner listening self is. This listening self is highly sensitive – both to other people's words and to other people's listening. Our inner listening contact with others allows us to communicate directly with the listening self of the other person, to receive them into the womb of our listening directly, and then to bear back to them what matures and ripens within this womb. This is true 'relating', for the original meaning of the word 'relate' is to 'bear back' (from the Latin *tollere* – to bear). Listening *is* the very essence of re-lating – our way of 'bearing with' another person and 'bearing back' what our soul receives from them.

The Listening Imagination

The way we 'bear with' another person, as we listen, bears back its own message – even without any spoken, verbal response. When we listen inwardly, the way we hear what someone is saying says something to them, the way we understand their words communicates wordlessly – for it is automatically 'borne back' to them. What is borne back to another person is in essence our inner bearing or comportment itself – not our physical posture but our inner listening posture. For it is our inner bearing as listeners that gives our hearing its own particular 'angle', one through which certain aspects of a person or situation come into view. If our listening attunement to another person is to be fruitful our inner bearing must be that of a patient midwife, attuned to what is still pregnant in silence. When a woman is pregnant she needs to adjust her physical posture and comportment in order to accommodate her big belly and her lowered centre of gravity. To adopt the inner bearing of the midwife is to lower the centre of gravity of our listening from the head and the heart to the hara, the soul-womb of our listening.

The inward expansion of this soul-womb can be compared to the inner expansion of dream space and dream time that occurs during sleep. We are generally as little conscious of our own listening self as we are of our dreaming self. The dreaming self, however, is not the *dreamt* self, the self we experience ourselves to be in our dreams. Our dreamt selves are like our spoken selves – the people we make ourselves out to be in our linguistic imagination. The dreaming self is the sleeping self that dreams – that is the source of our dreams and of our listening imagination. As we go to sleep, there is a point at which our <u>thoughts begin to be experienced as inner voices</u>, our <u>feelings as inner images.</u> We lose consciousness of physical space and time and enter dream space and dream time.

Often, when people feel their heads or hearts are full and that they can no longer listen, they get tired and begin to fall asleep. Yet it is precisely when our ordinary listening tires and we get sleepy that we come to the threshold of a deeper level of listening linked to the hara. If, instead of 'switching off' when our heads are full, we allow ourselves instead to sink into a more meditative type of listening, we

Dream State

19

can experience a process which is something like 'sleeping into' the words of others and 'dreaming' their inner meaning with our listening imagination. The images we behold may not be visually sharp or colourful, but they are substantial – for they are imbued with inner feeling and 'in-tuition' (literally: 'inner sight'). They are not images 'in' the head, but impressions of the soul. They are not 'in' us at all. Instead we are within them, feeling and understanding them *from* within. In this they are like images of our dreams, images which we can feel ourselves into as well as perceive from without.

The listening imagination is cultivated by practicing the recall of dreams. Both the images of a dream and the words with which we describe them are like elements of a map. Ordinary maps show the topology of physical space. In our speaking and dreaming we mark out the topology of soul-space. This is a 'hermeneutic' space or 'meaning space'. When we know we have just had a dream but cannot recall any images, we can do so in the following manner. First we need to identify and stay in touch with the particular soul-mood that lingers in us from the dream, its unique feeling quality. By attuning our inward listening to the feeling tone of the dream, we tune our feeling – our heart – to the overall 'region' of soul-space or 'meaning space' which the dream mapped out. The next step is to explore the topology of this region by small movements of the focal point or 'assemblage point' of our listening – the still-point of silence in the belly. Whenever, with this fine-tuning of the hara, we touch upon a point in soul-space which we had previously transformed into a dream image, the latter will once again surface in our consciousness. This is so because we are already within these images again – we have found the 'place' in our souls from which they emerged, the inner bearing from which they originally came into view. The subtle changes of our inner 'position' and subtle alteration of our inner 'bearing' which we use to recall a dream can be compared to movements of the foetus within the womb.

Recall of the details of a dream often occurs spontaneously when we begin to describe it or write it down in words. But only if we allow the exact words we choose for this description to come to mind spontaneously themselves. If our language itself is spontaneous it will not reshape, distort, embroider or interpret the dream (for a dream, like a story, can be told in many ways and with many different words). Instead it will convey the basic feeling tones of the dream and represent the exact positions or 'coordinates' of soul-space from which each dream image emerged. Both speaking and dreaming are ways of mapping the topology of soul-space. We can recall our dreams accurately, however, only if we do not superimpose our linguistic imagination on our dream imagination, but instead let our words arise from our listening attunement. In this way we cultivate a 'feeling memory' of our dreams and a sensitive use of language to describe them. The fine-tuning of the hara is a capacity to 'move' within the wordless and imageless 'meaning space' of our souls. Many people think they have no dreams, simply because they do not remember them. Others think they are 'bad' at remembering dreams, simply because they put no effort into this – and do not know what sort of effort and skill it requires. That is because ours is a waking culture and a speaking culture rather than a dreaming culture and a listening culture. We teach children to speak and write as best we can, but the capacity for deep listening takes as little priority in this culture and in our educational system as the capacity to recall dreams.

The psychology of the modern West places value on the *birth* of conscious feelings and thoughts from the 'dark' womb of the mind, brain and 'unconscious'. It does not value the process of 'going under' and learning to silently explore this darkness with our listening. Instead this is seen as a 'regression' to the womb or worse – as a journey to 'lower' realms of the soul and an 'underworld' of sexuality, chaos, darkness or 'evil'. Such myths begin as meaningful dreams themselves, but their images then become stock symbols and 'archetypes' of the linguistic (and psycho-analytic) imagination. The soul-spaces these myths map out are replaced by mythological stories themselves, which become 'tourist maps' for the psyche. They substitute for the cultivation of our own listening imagination in much the same way as Tele-visual images substitute for those which we generate ourselves when we listen to the radio or read a book.

The Freudian story of the 'unconscious' is a modern myth rooted in ancient ones which described an underworld of untrammelled instinctual drives and powers. But the way we experience this underworld has changed. What in the past – and in all spiritual traditions – was seen as a healing journey of return to the silent and wordless core of our being is something that confronts modern man in a different guise – as unwelcome 'depression'. The depressive process is in fact a healing one through which we allow ourselves to sink down again into our own wordless depths. There we can re-link (*re-legio*) with our source of inner strength – the hara. But there is no concept of hara in Western culture. Instead we speak of being 'up' or 'high' on the one hand (seen as 'good' or 'positive') or 'down' and 'low' on the other (seen as negative). We talk of 'depth of character' but at the same time seek spiritual heights and 'highs', elevation and uplift, and avoid our spiritual depths. Our entry to these depths is then forced on us by physical, intellectual or emotional 'lows'.

Just as current concepts of feeling are dominated by the false duality of 'up' and 'down', so are current concepts of character dominated by the false duality of 'extroversion' and 'introversion'. The outward-looking ego and the progressive expansion of the social economy is counter-posed to a contracted regressive, inward-looking ego or economy. The expansion of the soul is experienced as inflation of the ego or economy. Its contraction is felt as ego-loss or worthlessness and is symbolised by monetary deflation. In order to avoid cycles of mania and depression, the head has to morally monitor or control ego inflation, just as, to avoid cycles of boom and bust, the state must monitor and control monetary inflation. But cycles of outward expansion and inward contraction, ego inflation and ego deflation continue. This is because there is no concept anymore of the *inward expansion* of the economy or of the soul – of the soul as the womb of the ego. Nor is there any concept of psychological 'digestion', the break down of the psyche's products and their recycling. The process by which we mull our experience over and allow it to come to rest within us, so that we can gradually break it down and absorb its meaning, is a recycling process. Like eating, this process begins in the head and works downwards to the belly, where experience is 'spiritualised' in the hara. In physiological terms the movement that facilitates the digestive recycling process is called peristalsis. Head thinking is based on the opposite process – the speech process. This is a 'reverse peristalsis' in which we 'bring things up' from within, shaping them into recognisable linguistic units – words and sentences – which in turn provide 'food for thought'. But to speak, we must first listen and digest. The 'thinking of the belly' is a 'digestive' thinking, one which gives time for conscious thoughts and experience to sink down into the belly of the soul where its meaning can be digested and where answers to our questions can incubate over time. What is called 'stress', on the other hand, is the effect of experiences and 'food for thought' that go undigested within the hara – leading to both irritable bowels and irritable words.

Somatic, psychosomatic and mental health problems arise from disturbances in the relation of the three centres, head, heart and hara. Neurotic anxiety is a disturbance of the relation between head and heart resulting from a lack of inner strength and groundedness in the hara. Neurotic depression is a disturbance in the relation of heart and hara in which we experience our feeling life pulled down to a 'low' by our spiritual centre of gravity or pushed (de-pressed) by our thoughts. Psychotic states involve a severance or splitting of one or more centres. Schizophrenic states express a separation of head from heart and hara. Manic states express a separation of head and heart from the hara. Psychotic depression is the flip side of this – a state of entrapment in the isolated and split off hara centre, whose womb is then experienced as a tomb.

Hara, Voice and the Art of Listening

All mental health problems are themselves the flip side of conflicting or one-sided cultural concepts of health. Western culture is oriented around the head and the heart. The intellect sees the emotions as untrustworthy and in need of control, the heart as weak and vulnerable. This does not reflect the true strength and wisdom of our feeling life but its lack of groundedness in the hara. It is this that makes our emotional life volatile and unpredictable, susceptible to thoughts and over-dependent on reason or thought control for its stability. The head acknowledges only feelings which it is able to verbally label and pigeon-hole in its lexicon of 'emotions' – anger, sadness, love, hate etc. Music, on the other hand, is a pure language of feeling tone and transcends the limited vocabulary of the emotions. Hence its healing value – but only if we are first able to listen.

The fundamental pathology of our age is not aids or cancer, stress or depression, neuroticism or psychosis – it is the repression of our spiritual centre and the resulting incapacity to listen. To listen is to create a receptive listening space in the region under the head and the heart, the intellect and emotions. To 'under-stand' is quite literally to hear from 'under' or below – from the still-point of silence in the hara. The hara is both the belly and inner womb of our listening. Listening is our way of dwelling within it. By rooting our listening in the hara and making contact with others from it, we automatically help others to listen to themselves more deeply, to listen from their own hara and learn to speak from it. We learn to *hear* where people are speaking 'from' – whether from the head, heart or hara.

The Japanese term *hara-goe* refers to 'the voice coming from the belly' which, as Graf Dürckheim points out:

> ....is valued as an expression of integrated wholeness and total presence....If a man utters profound truths from the larynx, the Japanese do not trust him. They consider him insincere.

A speaking that issues purely from the head and intellect has a quite different tone and 'voice' than one which arises purely from the heart, from the hara, or from a complex combination of these three.

The speech of the individual is a per-sonal ('through-sound') expression of their soul constitution – the inner relation between head, heart and hara. If a person's speaking is not a listening speech, a speech centred in the hara, its tone lacks inner spaciousness or resonance – however rich or resonant their voice tones may be. Inner tone has to do not just with vocal tones, but with the tempo and articulation of their speech – and with the tone of their language. For when we read an author we detect a certain 'tone' in their language which is quite distinct from vocal tone. The presence or absence of *hara-goe*, therefore is not merely a question of whether someone's voice comes from the throat, the chest or the belly. We can also hear where a person's words come from – 'off the top of their head', 'from the heart' or from a wordless inner knowing 'an understanding that precedes words'. The listening imagination is a powerful 'diagnostic' medium, allowing us to get an intuitive and feeling 'picture' of the soul-body of another person and its particular constitution – the characteristic relation and relative weighting of head, heart and hara that the individual embodies in their way of speaking.

'Personality' is the way we bear our souls forth in speech. 'Character' is the way we bear our souls within us in silence. The fact that someone does not speak from the heart does not mean they do not feel, that they are not silently in touch with their heart. The same is true of head and hara. The listening imagination allows us to hear the unspoken voice of the individual – to touch the centres that find no voice. By establishing an inner contact and communication with these centres through both our words and our silence, we stimulate them into life, responding not only to the outer personality of the individual but to their inner character.

The 'genealogy' of character has to do with the way we each come to be who we are. Its true basis is not our genes or environment but the way we come to words and they to us. 'Genea-logy' refers to the *genesis* of the word or *logos* within us, to the way we listen to ourselves before we speak. The fact that today drinking whisky can be advertised under the slogan 'a measure of character' is a sign of our times. Alcohol has become the principle means by which people seek to liberate themselves from the thinking of the head and heart. Spirits are bought as a way to overcome the repression of spirit. But the gut feelings that these bring up from the belly – along with other things – have little to do with depth of character, or with the 'inner voice' of the hara.

In the past, Samurai warriors schooled in Zen would deliberately tie their belts an inch or so below the navel in order to anchor their awareness in the *tanden* – the physical focal point of the hara. In this way it became a source of inner strength and physical power. The *tanden* was referred to simply (and misleadingly) as 'the thing below the navel'. Today 'hara' and 'tanden' are subjects for Zen scholars rather than warriors. In the future I hope their function will not be the empowerment of the physical body in the martial arts, but the empowerment of the soul through the art of listening.

The Japanese term *Haragei* refers to any human activity or art form engaged in from the hara as well as the head and heart. Both Japanese *Haiku* and European *Lieder* (sung poetry) are forms of *Haragei*. To sing *Lieder* well, to communicate the words of a poem and imbue them with musical feeling through her voice, the singer requires not only a particularly composed physical comportment. She must also find the appropriate 'inner bearing' – using her listening imagination to find the place within her soul which the words and music of the *Lied* touch. This is a silent and wordless place between heart and hara. From it inner images and feeling tones can arise on which her words and vocal tones can ride. Only by singing from her inward listening imagination can she fully embody and bear forth the inner bearing, and inner mood and 'inner voice' of the poet – not only in her singing but in the silent yet pregnant pauses of her voice. To do so she must also be able to breathe with the soul-belly (*psyche* = 'breath'), to let its inner feeling tones ring out and reverberate in the air, touching us in our souls.

The poet knows how easy it is to get 'hooked on language', to let the intuitive listening imagination get carried away by the linguistic imagination. The purpose of poetry is not to re-present experience in words but to communicate the immediate presencing of something essentially wordless. It is our listening intent, not our linguistic imagination, which first lets things be said, bids and beckons them into presence. What comes to presence through the poem is not any verbal concept, meaning or image, it is an 'idea' that gathers from our wordless and felt sense of meaning. An 'idea' in the original Greek sense (*eidos*), an 'appearance' that presences and brings to view the essence of what it manifests.

Thinking is a listening that brings something to view. Therefore in thinking both ordinary hearing and ordinary seeing pass away for us, for thinking brings about in us a listening and a bringing-into-view.

Martin Heidegger

Both poetry and song – as *Haragei* – bring about in us a 'listening and a bringing-into-view'. So too, can each encounter with another human being.

SOUL SCIENCE
The Listening Science
of the Psyche (Breath)

Introduction

To even use the term 'soul-science' seems questionable to the modern mind. We know – or think we know – what science is. But what is meant by 'soul'? Is there such a thing? Can it be 'proved'? These are philosophical questions which cannot be ignored. To understand what is meant by soul-science we need, if not to give final answers to these questions, at least to begin with them, to examine them more deeply.

To ask what anything *is* – 'soul' for example – is always and at the same time to ask what is meant by the word which names it – in this case the word 'soul' or the phrase 'the soul'. Believers and atheists may debate whether or not God exists. Yet to do so already assumes that we know what someone means when they talk about 'God', or 'the soul'. The personal meaning that words such as 'God', 'soul', 'heaven' or 'love' have for one person, a Christian for example, may be quite different from the meaning they have for a Jew, an atheist, or even another Christian of the same denomination. This applies not only to words but also to names such as 'Christ', 'Allah', 'Buddha' etc. The same words and names mean different things to different people. Indeed a given word or name may come to mean different things to the same person at different times. Conversely, similar meanings may be expressed using different words and names, not only by different people but also by the same person.

There is a gap, in other words, between meaning and its expression. This may seem like common sense, and yet from the viewpoint of modern linguistics, it isn't. At roughly the same time, historically, that materialist science and philosophy began to deny the independent reality of anything that could be called soul, the idea arose that meaning and thought were in no way separable from words and language. Linguists and linguistic philosophers argued that there can ultimately be no gap between meaning and its expression, for this would imply that meaning has a reality that precedes words. This argument is in essence quite circular, for it identifies meaning with words without acknowledging in any way that 'to mean' is also a verb, that meaning is something we do and not just a property of language.

Beings Who Mean

Whenever we use the phrase 'What do you mean by....?' we imply that it is people, human beings, who mean things. Meaning is not just something that words 'have', but something that human beings do. People mean something with their words, and with their gestures and actions. So, indeed, do animals. Most cat owners would agree that when their pet hovers around the food bowl, looking at its owner and *miouwing* it too means something. But when a computer displays or fails to display information, even when it asks us a question or composes a poem, this is precisely what is lacking. We may be delighted with the information, or be enraged by a glitch in the software. But the computer does not *mean* anything with it. It neither means any thing nor means any person. Instead it is *we* who find meaning in the information, and in the computer's functioning.

To ask about the meaning of the word 'soul' is therefore paradoxical. For only a being who means can mean something with this question, or mean something with the word 'soul'. Indeed, one way of defining 'a soul' is precisely this: a being who means. This is not the same thing as 'a being with consciousness'. Philosophers may argue about whether or not we can really prove that other people have conscious minds, when all we can perceive are their bodies and bodily actions (including the action of speaking). The same question can be raised about animals, plants or about the foetus in the womb. What is undeniable is that other beings 'mean' something to us – in both the active and passive senses of this phrase. Consciousness is not just consciousness of 'things', of objects, words, actions and events. It is also consciousness of meaning and of beings who mean.

But what do we mean by 'meaning'? Here again language itself comes to our aid in exploring this question. The verb 'to mean' is itself intrinsically self-referential. In everyday usage we speak of 'meaning' a particular 'meaning' or 'sense' – *intending* it. In expressions such as 'I didn't mean it', or, 'I didn't mean it that way', meaning defines itself as 'intending'. In questions such as 'What is the meaning of ...?' meaning defines itself as something which words or events 'have'. The same applies to questions of 'soul'. We can regard the soul as something we have – or don't have. Or we can regard it as something we do, as something that belongs to the realm of intentionality. 'A soul is a being who means', means in this sense, a soul is a being who *intends*.

Why give the name 'soul' to 'a being who means'? This, too, is a valid question, but one that again can only be answered by going more deeply into the question itself and listening more closely to its language. To ask 'why' is to seek one of two things – either a reason or cause on the one hand, and a meaning or intent on the other. When we ask someone 'why' they did or said something we are asking them to articulate their meaning or intent. Another way of putting this is to ask what the 'reason' or 'cause' of their statement or action was. But this is not quite the same thing. Lacking the right sort of 'reasons' people do things which others find irrational. Because of this we look for other 'causes' of their behaviour. Such is the way in which we approach anything that appears mad or bad in this world. What it denies, however, is any sense in which actions which appear to defy our standards of 'rationality' or 'goodness' may be the expression of good intentions – may be 'well-meant'. It denies the possibility of any gap between meaning and expression.

In the past it was not always so. There was a time when people did their best to regard all that befell them in life as part of 'God's plan'. Good because it was *meant* to be by God, and therefore also *well-*meant. Today, however, we confuse such trust in divine well-meaning with concepts of 'pre-determination' based on inexorable chains of causality. But meaning is not causality. Something that is well-meant can indeed turn out well or badly, depending on how we interpret and express this meaning. This in turn has to do with language, for it is through language that we represent and try to rationalise the meaning of our actions and of our lives. The fact that God means well – that there may be an inner meaning to events – does not guarantee that we will appreciate this inner meaning. Just as we may regard our dreams as 'irrational' or even 'bad', so we may also erect barriers that prevent us from seeing the inner meaning of life events. The psycho-analytic concept of the unconscious as a cesspool of 'primitive' uncontrolled aggressive and sexual drives may lead us to deny and fear the inner meaning of our dreams – and of our deeds – in the same way that earlier religious concepts of hell and of 'evil demons' led people to deny or fear their own 'souls' rather than finding meaning in them or seeking the good intent within them. As a result, words or behaviour that contradicted religious norms were treated as evil, and explained by demonic possession.

Nowadays we are less inclined to explain abnormal or 'evil' behaviour as the result of demonic possession, though Freud still implied a sort of possession by the 'unconscious drives'. 'Psychiatry' on the other hand looks for more 'scientific' explanations. A psychiatrist examining a 'mentally ill' patient with this approach may be full of heart-felt compassion for the individual concerned, as well as intellectually curious as to the reasons or causes of their irrational or unethical behaviour. And yet any approach to illness and suffering – mental or physical – based only on 'reasons' and 'causes' well-deserves the adjective 'soul-less', for it denies that mental and physical symptoms are in any way meant – and 'well-meant' – by the suffering individual.

When a 'being who means' cannot find words to represent and rationalise their own meanings and intents in a personally or socially acceptable way, then they are forced to take recourse to alternative languages – to develop physical symptoms or to behave or speak in ways that make no sense to others. To find the meaning of physical or behavioural symptoms is impossible unless we grant that there is a meaning. This is not the same thing as looking for reasons and causes. Looking for reasons and causes may help us to locate a fault in a computer or piece of software. Indeed a computer can itself be programmed to check and correct its own functioning in this way. Discovering a person's meaning and intent is another matter however. Only a being who means can listen to what is meant by another being. Put in other words – it takes one to know one. Only as beings of soul – beings who mean – can we perceive the inner reality of soul, the reality of inner meaning.

Accepting the reality of soul is no more difficult than accepting the gap between meaning on the one hand and its expression in word, image and deed on the other. Identifying meaning with reasons and causes is like explaining a piece of music with physics, and the feelings it evokes with brain waves and body chemistry. To look for the origins of consciousness in the body makes no more sense than to look for the meaning of words by analysing the ink on the written page or the sound-waves of speech. The soul dwells in the world in the same way that meaning dwells in the word – invisibly and inaudibly. The sounds of music only mean something because the composer – a being – means something *through* them.

In speaking, people mean something *dia-logos*: 'through the word'. Whenever we speak we are in dialogue not just through language but also with language. The meanings that words themselves 'have' accrue from all the ways that they have been meant by human beings in the past. And yet whenever a common word is used again, it is imbued not just with given meanings inherited from past speakers but with a fresh 'speaker's meaning' – the meaning that the new speaker gives to it. Linguistics assumes that verbal communication is only possible if the senses that words convey are common ones – agreed and shared by everyone. True 'common sense' knows otherwise. It knows that we don't understand the other person when we understand their words merely in terms of common and agreed meanings but when we understand the personal meaning which the speaker imbues them with. We may not be able to articulate such personal differences of meaning in the same way that we define common or agreed meanings of language. But if we listen, we can hear them wordlessly.

How is it possible for us to hear meanings 'in our souls' that are not identical with word meanings, but are nevertheless conveyed through them? 'Scientific' explanation would have us believe that we do this purely through perceptual information – eye-signals and body language, for example. This is like saying that when lovers gaze into each other's eyes and feel themselves to be gazing into each other's souls what they are doing is examining each other's pupils and eye movements and 'interpreting' these as signals. Common sense, again, tells us otherwise. We know that as soon as we begin to optically inspect each other's eyes there is no longer any real 'eye contact'. Eye-contact is contact between two beings, both of whom mean something *through* their gaze and feel themselves meant through the gaze of the other. If I am looking at your eyes I am looking at a thing but not at a being – I am not looking at *you*. And if it is merely my *eye* that examines you then *I* am not looking at you – not meaning you with my gaze. Indeed to look at a person in a way that makes genuine eye-contact requires us *not* to focus our vision on their eyes as such but on a point between and behind the eyes.

The radiance, light and darkness of someone's gaze is not physical light, however brightly it may seem to shine and however much it brightens what it rests on. Ordinary science has no physics to explain the trans-physical qualities of this gaze-light, any more than it can explain the trans-physical qualities of movement communicated through gesture and dance, the trans-physical qualities of form and colour communicated through painting, or the trans-physical qualities of sound communicated through music, song and speech.

When a mother hears her baby crying or gazes at it in the cot, it is indeed her baby that she hears and not a mere sound; her baby that she looks at, not a pair of eyes. In touching and handling her baby, she touches and handles a *being*, not a body that her baby 'has'.

34

When the baby cries, chuckles or babbles it is not indirectly re-presenting or 'coding' meanings in sounds. It is presencing its being quite directly 'through sound': *per-sonally*. The word persona refers to the masks worn by actors in classical Greek drama, the faces through which they sounded forth. Responding *personally* to the baby, the mother will not only echo these sounds but give them a face, expressing with her look the feeling tones that they communicate.

What does the baby see when he or she looks at the mother's face. I am suggesting that, ordinarily, what the baby sees is himself or herself. In other words, the mother is looking at the baby and *what she looks like is related to what she sees there.* Winnicott

The mother's look expresses her way of looking at and seeing the baby. If she is in tune with the baby it will also mirror back the feeling tones communicated by the baby's sounds and face. In essence, however, the mother does not attune to the baby's feelings but to her baby as such. The feeling tones that she 'mirrors' and gives form to in her face are the very wavelengths of attunement linking her to the baby as a being. The mother does not first perceive the baby as an object, then decode its language to find meaning, and finally respond by representing her own meaning in sounds and body language. Her very way of listening to and looking at the baby, of hearing and seeing it, itself says something to the baby, bearing back its own meaning and personifying this meaning. Winnicott calls this perceptual interaction of mother and baby 'apperception' to distinguish it from a subjective act of perception that turns the perceived being into a soul-less object of perception. But what happens to babies, Winnicott asks, if the mother is not attuned to the baby, if the mother's face or voice merely reflects her own mood, or 'worse still, the rigidity of her own defences'?

....the baby gets settled into the idea that when he or she looks, what is seen is the mother's face....perception takes the place of apperception, of that which might have been the beginning of a significant exchange with the world, a two-way process in which self-enrichment alternates with the discovery of meaning in the world of seen things.

This, in a nutshell, is the viewpoint of natural science, which regards nature like the face of the unattuned and unresponsive mother, not as a mirror and echo of the soul, but as a face to be studied, read and interpreted.

Some babies do not quite give up hope and they study the object and do all that is possible to see in the object some meaning that ought to be there if only it could be felt. (Others) study the maternal visage in an attempt to predict the mother's mood, just exactly as we all study the weather. Winnicott

Ordinary science studies the maternal 'visage' of the world – representing it with theories and formulae, words and images, numbers and diagrams. 'Truth' becomes a property attached to language and representational knowledge and not to our immediate, personal and felt sense of what things mean to us. The meaning of a word, or thing is simply its conventional, shared meaning – not what it means to us or what we mean with it. The relation between meaning and being is thereby broken. We no longer understand that for something to *be* for us and be what it *is* for us is the same thing as meaning something to us and/or being meant by us in a certain way. The essence or 'beingness' of things – their 'soul' – is what they mean to us in our being. Therefore to really *be* with someone fully is to respond to what they mean to us in our being by meaning them as beings – not treating the other merely as an 'it' or object. This applies not just to persons but to things. We can treat a thing, the sea for example, as an object or as something with beingness and meaning – with 'soul'. We can listen to it and hear 'waves breaking'. Or we can hear waves speaking. We can look at the face of mother nature – or we can meet its gaze.

We do not find meaning lying in things
nor do we put it into things,
but between us and things it can happen.

Martin Buber

Language, Genes and Soul

As souls we are beings who mean other beings and are also meant by other beings. We are beings who mean something to other beings and we are beings for whom other beings mean something. But the world of commerce and science is governed by an essentially soul-less technological language, one in which information replaces meaning and beings are treated as mere objects of planning and calculation. Words such as *user, system, stock, resource, market, skill and productivity* all belong to this language. In it 'the world' means only the worldwide market for labour, currencies and commodities. The earth is seen as no more than a stock of exploitable human and mineral reserves. Human beings too are managed and disposed of as 'human resources', treated as mere assemblages of functional and tradable 'skills'. As for plants and animals, these are seen simply as live-stocks of genetic raw materials. The tree is merely a biological timber producer or fruit factory. The sea is a vast fish farm or a saleable tourist commodity.

With computer technology the meaningful perceptual interaction of infant and mother becomes the man-monitor interface; 'interaction' consists solely of 'inputs' and 'outputs' of information, and 'dialogue' refers only to 'dialogue boxes' demanding yes-no decisions by the user. The computer with its 'motherboard' is indeed a 'virtual' mother – one available at all times for 'hands on' contact, one that can frustrate or satisfy with its occasional unpredictability, but one that ultimately can be mastered, controlled – 'programmed' to satisfy the user's needs and even reflect the user's image and personality.

Four main types of discourse have replaced the previous language of soul: psychological discourse, biological discourse, ethical discourse and 'neo-spiritual' discourse. The soul is memorialised in the terms 'psychology', 'psychiatry' and 'psychoanalysis', all stemming from the Greek *psyche*. And yet none of these disciplines speaks of the soul, but instead of the 'mind', 'brain' or 'the unconscious'. Alternatively, as in 'post-modern' thinking and Lacanian psychoanalysis, the psyche is understood entirely on the basis of a particularly soul-less intellectual concept of language, developed only in the modern age.

Biological language sees living beings not as 'beings who mean' but merely as instruments serving the survival of the fittest genes. The immortal gene replaces the immortal soul. Genetic structure is understood as a biological code or language. But genetic science does not acknowledge how genes, no less than words, not only serve our physical life and self-expression but are vehicles of expression for trans-physical potentials of being – for 'values' and 'meanings'.

What we call 'soul' is the other side of what we call 'language' – the broader and deeper dimension of language which has to do with our entire life of meaning and with our essential being. Verbal language cannot be separated from 'language' in this deeper 'metaphorical' sense – our capacity as beings to mean – in whatever way meaning is expressed. Nor can meaning be separated from being – from who we each *are*. Each of us not only 'has' or 'speaks' a language. Each of us also *is* a language. The language that we *are* is our whole 'language of being' – our unique way of meaning. Just as each artist speaks to us in their own unique language, irrespective of their formal medium or style, so does each person express themselves in their own unique way, one which transcends common features such as language, dialect and idiom. Not only their way of speaking but their whole way of looking and listening, working and playing, thinking and feeling, is itself a unique idiom, a 'way of meaning' which we understand, like art, through its aesthetic.

The word 'language' acknowledges all the ways in which, as beings, we *mean* things to one another. The word 'soul' acknowledges the truth that all meanings are ultimately the expression, not of cosmic forces or chance, but of beings who mean. As beings we are not bound to express ourselves in any particular language – including the languages of bodyhood, of physical existence and perception. All languages in which we do express ourselves including the shared biological language of genes and bodyhood are translations of our essential languages of being. The ethical dilemmas raised by genetic engineering and bio-technology, like those connected with the relative significance of 'heredity' and 'environment' in individual development, are a classic example of the failure to understand both biological and verbal languages as languages of the soul, as expressions of 'beings who mean'. What we call 'genes' are shared physical potentials, expressing themselves as physical features and capacities. What we call 'values' are shared potentials of being. These express themselves as qualities and capacities of soul, as characteristic ways of meaning. The ethical language of 'values' and the biological language of 'genetics' have common roots in our very nature as meaning beings. As we grow up we translate our genetic potentials into bodily features and functions. We also translate our potentials of being – our values – into qualities and capacities of soul – characteristic ways of meaning. The keyword here is 'translation'. Just as it is difficult to pin down biologically the physical features and functions expressed by a particular gene, so it is difficult to pin down in language the essential values expressed by particular qualities and capacities of soul.

Physical resemblances give us a way of labelling and accounting for each other's physical features – 'so-and-so' has his mother's eyes, his father's nose etc. And yet (s)he doesn't – for every nose and every pair of eyes is unique, every body a unique combination of genes. The same is true of soul-resemblances – we construe them in terms of family, race, religion or culture, and yet we are each unique combinations of soul-qualities. An individual may strike you as particularly honest or sincere, and yet the particular quality of their 'honesty' or 'sincerity' is unique – subtly different from those of other people you know who share the same qualities. Words such as 'honesty', 'sincerity', 'integrity' and 'loyalty' are an attempt to name the essential 'spiritual' values expressed through these soul-qualities.

Genetic potentials are activated by the migration and interaction of cells in the growing body, and by the cellular environments they find themselves in. 'Spiritual-genes' – inner values or potentials of being – are activated by the migration and interaction of people, and the physical and social environments they find themselves in. Whether a particular biological gene finds expression depends partly on its genetic, cellular environment, and partly on the external physical environment of the body. At the same time, whether an individual manages to embody a particular value depends partly on the 'value climate' of their social environment.

Values and genes are not merely analogous to one another, but linked in reality. Values are not only inherited through religious and cultural languages, but through the language of our genes themselves. Like genes, they are 'written' in our physical constitution. How we embody these 'written' values in our character or 'way of being' and how we express and personify these values in our speech and behaviour – in our 'way of meaning'– are both influenced by our family and cultural environment, in the same way that our physical environment influences the activation of our genes. But the family is *itself* a physical environment – an environment of bodies and not just of minds. The moral tone and climate in which a child is brought up is not determined by the parental *mind* alone – by the parents' beliefs or moral codes. It is also shaped by the parents' 'body language' – their characteristic demeanour. The moods, mannerisms and 'masks' which make up our physical demeanour, themselves embody a particular ethical bearing. Our demeanour is the way in which we translate our innermost values into qualities of soul and 'ways of meaning', not by verbalising them but by embodying them in our physical comportment, gestures and countenance. Demeanour links our own physical constitution and genetic heritage with our ethical bearing and the values it expresses. Ethical bearing is embodied in physical postures – for example the 'upright' posture of Victorian morality or the 'laid back' stance of Californian liberalism.

The words 'ethics' and 'morality' originally referred to the characteristic spirit and customs of a people – to their *ethos* and *mores*. *Mores* derives from *mos* – a way of carrying or bearing oneself – from which we also derive the word 'morose'. Morose implies silent, mute or brooding – bearing something within oneself. The characteristic way in which individuals in a particular culture 'bear themselves' embodies their *mores*. Character is the way we bear ourselves in silence. Personality on the other hand, is the way we bear ourselves forth in speech. In speech we personify our inner bearing in our facial mask or *persona*, and in the moral tones and gestures which 'sound through' (*per-sonare*) this mask. Demeanour links character and personality: our way of bearing ourselves in silence and our way of communicating this inner bearing in gestures and tones of speech. Demeanour expresses both our way of being in our bodies and relating to our genetic heritage, and our way of meaning something through our bodies and thereby embodying our innermost values or potentials of being.

The ethical meaning of interactions between members of a family has everything to do with demeanour. The demeanour of the child means something to the parent and vice versa. A parent who seeks to impart certain values to the child without embodying these in his or her demeanour is bound to fail. A parent who judges and criticises the demeanour of a child without acknowledging the values that the child seeks to embody through it will fail. Through miming the demeanour of parents children find an initial way of embodying and expressing their own values. Subtle family resemblances and differences in physical appearance reveal different aspects of the family gene pool. Subtle family resemblances and differences in demeanour represent different ways of embodying and expressing the *value pool* from which each member of the family draws – its pool of potentialities, including creative gifts and talents.

As adults we may still feel ourselves saddled with moods, mannerisms and 'masks' which mimic a *familiar* demeanour – that of a parent, or of a relative or sibling. This may only come to our notice when we ourselves become parents. Suddenly we find ourselves relating to our children as our parents related to us, whilst at the same time we begin to understand within ourselves what the demeanour of a particular parent actually meant – what it embodied and expressed. We may choose partners who seem to embody a familiar demeanour, who bring it out in us. Alternatively our own demeanour may be such as to bring out its family *counterpart* in a child or partner.

These processes fall under the heading of 'transference' in psychoanalysis. Transference can mean relating to others as our parents related to us, or as we related to them. Essentially it means relating to ourselves as our parents related to themselves. Transference is often understood as a process which reproduces destructive family relationships in new relationships and families. But a relationship free of transference is neither possible nor creative.

Transference is not what is commonly called 'projection' or 'projective identification', for we do not need to project anything onto someone's demeanour in order for this demeanour to *mean* something to us, for every human demeanour is an individual way of embodying and expressing common human feelings and values. To relate is to 're-late' – to 'bear back' (re-latio) – the common feelings and values that are embodied in another person's demeanour in one's own way, to translate them into a demeanour of one's own. Our original family relationships are *themselves* transferences in this sense – translations of parental demeanour in our own terms. Only by understanding transference as translation do we acknowledge its creative character and allow ourselves also to turn it into something creative.

Just as nobody has identical features to a parent, even where resemblances are marked, so nobody, least of all a child, 'merely' imitates and reproduces the demeanour of parents. Something is always added and altered in the process. Every individual embodies unique combinations of genes from the family pool, not all of which show up in the parents. Similarly, each child embodies in its demeanour unique combinations of values from the value pool of the family – not all of which mimic the demeanour of parents or siblings.

In relating to its parents and 'bearing back' the values embodied in the adult's demeanour, the child not only learns to embody and express values which the parent already embodies and expresses, but begins a long process of translating these values into its own 'language of being' and combining them with other values which form part of the family pool. The genetic pool of a family includes genes and gene combinations which no single, living member of the family as yet embodies. Similarly, the 'value atmosphere' of a family or group includes dis-carnate values and value combinations, some of which can find expression only *through* the particular genetic constitution of one specific member of the family. Individual value fulfilment is connected both with the acknowledgement of shared 'family values' *and* of specific combinations of these values which endow the individual with gifts – 'potentials of being'– that no other member of the family can embody in quite the same way. These are written into the individual's genes, and can be 'read' in their bodily character, even though they may at first find no expression in the mind and personality of the individual.

Like bad weather, the value climate of the family, with its clouds and storms, can discourage the expression of potentials present in the overall value atmosphere. At the same time such storms may be necessary to clear the atmosphere – allowing an inner soul-light and soul-warmth to shine through and illuminate these values. The moral education of children is connected with the parents' awareness and understanding of the value atmosphere and value climate within which the child grows up. This includes not just the atmosphere and climate of the family itself but of larger communities and society as a whole.

Religion, Science and Moral-Education

Parents and teachers may pay attention to social issues such as unemployment, crime and drugs, but ignore the spiritual and soul-dimensions of individual value fulfilment. Religious educators seek to promote spiritual values through the written and spoken word. Scientists and intellectuals argue about the respective role of genes and environment in criminal and 'anti-social' behaviour. While sport and physical activities may be encouraged as an antidote to this behaviour, no-one anymore acknowledges (as they did in Victorian times) that spiritual values are intimately linked with the soul of the child's body – that they are channelled through its physical bearing and countenance, physical posture and demeanour. The language of moral character is replete with body language: we speak of moral 'backbone', a friendly 'gesture' or 'posture', a compassionate 'stance', to 'shoulder' responsibility or lend a 'hand' etc. Yet educators stick to the idea that moral education begins with the word rather than the body. Perhaps the opposite is the case – namely that moral *talk* and discussion should be the *last* stage in moral education and 'character development'. What it should begin with is an exploration of the inner tone and character of particular bodily stances and gestures. Through these the child can develop a sense of how each stance and gesture embodies or expresses a particular inner bearing – a way of relating to themselves, to others and to the world. If, for example,

....an open armed, hospitable stance is really crucial for the full exercising of our moral nature; if in fact it is the very incarnation, an exemplary incarnation, of our capacity for moral relationship, then the teaching of this stance, and its open armed gesture, must surely be essential. And it must also be the very best way to teach our children the understanding feeling - the deeply felt meaning - of some basic moral precepts.   David Levin

Levin suggests a two phased pedagogical practice:

In the first phase, the children are shown that stance and gesture, and invited to replicate it for themselves in a situation which suffices to make it clear as constitutive of a relationship with others....Finally, after many brief sessions of practice, the teacher slowly and patiently begins to speak to them of the moral attributes they are already bodying forth, and helps them to feel, by their focussing - feel, that is to say, with their bodies - the progressively well-rooted *physiognomic meaningfulness* of these moral attributes.

The purpose of drama education is to cultivate an inner appreciation of the physiognomic meaningfulness of bodily demeanour, gestures and comportment. This is essential to cultivating a child's ability to mean – not just to speak and use words properly but to embody his or her inner, felt sense of meaning. Only in this way can the child come to feel that he or she already is 'some-body', without having to prove this through intellectual, academic or athletic achievement.

Music appreciation, too, is central to the education of the child's emotional, philosophical and moral sensibility – far more so than lessons devoted to artificially prompted intellectual debates on ethical or philosophical issues. Through the cultivation of musical listening, a child learns to distinguish between verbally labelled emotions on the one hand, and the otherwise nameless *tones of feeling* that only music can properly echo and convey. Feeling tones are neither audible tones of sound, nor are they emotions which can be verbally labelled. They are the very wavelengths of attunement that link us 'empathically' with others and allow us also to appreciate musical tones. Music reminds us that the pre-verbal dimension of meanings is far from being undifferentiated. The music of feeling tone is a language as rich and differentiated as music, for it is an 'inner music' of feeling tone. Feeling tone is the most intrinsically meaningful dimension of our being, for it is the primordial medium through which beings mean, intend, and intend meanings. Intention is itself a type of silent inner tonation – expressed both in vocal intonation and musical tonality.

Audible music is intrinsically meaningful to the soul because it emerges from the silent inner music of the soul. The composer too, begins by listening inwardly to tones of silence and translating these tones of silence into music that he or she hears inwardly. The composition is itself a listening response to this inner music, the music from which we all constantly compose and re-compose ourselves. It also learns to distinguish between stereotyped spiritual values named and codified through the written word – in religious texts, for example – and the nameless wealth of moral tones communicated through music. Words such as 'nobility', 'grandeur', 'strength' and 'pathos' only hint at the totally unique and true nature of these moral tones, which, unlike words and abstract moral concepts, are at the same time imbued with great personal feeling. We are used to thinking of 'moral tone' only in terms of the voice – the speaker's tone – and in two dimensions – 'high' or 'low'. The moral tones of a parent or teacher link their tone of voice to the use of certain types of moral language and the exercise of moral judgments. In music, on the other hand, rich symphonic architecture of feeling tone and moral tone is intrinsically 'democratic' – expressing different voices and aspects of the self. Emotional and moral questions are not posed and resolved intellectually or emotionally but in the soul – tonally and musically.

To identify 'moral education' with the written word or with discussion of moral and emotional issues is one sided. It addresses the heads and hearts of children but not their soul. Nor does it develop the listening sensitivity of soul that alone makes human dialogue meaningful. It may seem that listening to a piece of music and listening to people talk are far apart. But when we listen to a symphony we are also listening to people – to the composer, conductor and orchestra. It may take several hearings of a piece of music for us to appreciate and enjoy it to the full. To begin with our listening is blank. As a result we hear only sounds. We hear these sounds as music only when we hear and play this music internally with the chords and harmonies of our own feeling tones. Listening as such – whether to music, to nature, to our own thoughts and feelings or to other people – is essentially musical. It not only requires and cultivates 'self-composure', it is the way we quite literally compose and de-compose, unite and differentiate the inner moral tones of our feelings, the inner music of our souls.

When we listen to poetry, drama or song, we hear how speech rides on musical patterns of vocal intonation and modulates these patterns – using them as carrier waves to impart information. And just as messages of great intellectual sophistication and ethical meaning can ride on the carrier waves of vocal intonation, so can music itself be the bearer of profound philosophical and ethical wisdom – quite literally a medium of spiritual teaching. The idea that music is something to be taught needs to be balanced by the understanding that music itself is a medium of teaching. It is an irony of our times that children and adults who read books of great intellectual, scientific or even spiritual sophistication still listen to the musical equivalent of comic books or cartoons – that they are not able to appreciate and 'read' great works of music in the same way as great literature. The 'astounding' discovery that playing certain types of classical music in lessons can improve children's mathematical skills comes as no surprise to musicians and musicologists. Musical intelligence transcends the false division of intellectual and emotional intelligence, mathematical forms and human meanings. Different types of music demand and cultivate different ways of listening. They cultivate the listening intelligence and listening imagination of both adults and children toward the listening soul. Spiritual teaching is teaching that lets us learn something from our own souls. Great works of music, no less than works of philosophy, have the effect of truly spiritual teachings – they let us hear the speech of our own souls, riding on its inner music.

Meaning, Metaphor and Mysticism

The language of 'soul' introduced in this work, including terms such as 'soul-science' and 'soul-music' will be dismissed by the scientific mind as 'mere' metaphor or analogy. Yet scientific discourse itself abounds in overt or covert metaphor, like 'to weigh' the evidence, or 'carry out' research. Without metaphor there would be no abstract thought at all. To 'ab-stract' meant originally to 'pull away from' (Latin *ab-strahere*). The modern meaning of the word has itself been 'pulled away from' this original sense – one we no longer hear – but remains rooted in it.

An expression such as 'to *hold* someone in one's memory' is one amongst countless examples of bodily metaphors used in everyday language. It seems to abstract something from the physical and bodily sense which it then bears into a psychic dimension. But are we to assume from this metaphorical usage that psychically 'holding' someone in one's memory is therefore less 'real' or more 'abstract' than physically holding a photograph in our hands? Perhaps the opposite is true – perhaps we hold the photograph of someone in our hands to express in a bodily and material manner the way that we cherish them in our memory. Perhaps we speak of 'holding' someone in our memory in order to quite literally give flesh to our meaning, to give it an almost tangible bodily sense. The basic principle here is not one of abstraction – 'lifting' a physical sense and turning it into something metaphysical. It is the reverse. We begin with a tangible, 'almost' physical sense of a psychic state or process – a meaning we wish to convey. We then embody this 'pre-physical' sense in one of two ways – either by doing something with our bodies (picking up and holding the photograph) or using bodily language to give flesh to it. The metaphorical process does not start with the realm of physical action and language and then use or abuse it to describe other realms. It ends with physical action and language, which are themselves the metaphors of 'pre-physical' meanings, sensations and processes.

The world of meaning is not an 'abstract' world devoid of sensation, feeling, movement or action – any more than is the world of dream experience. In dreaming we symbolise our inner, felt sense of meaning with physical images and events. We symbolise movements in the sensual inner 'meaning space' of our feelings as

47

movements in physical space. We do the same in speaking – translating 'soul-senses', 'soul-events', and 'soul-movements' into words which have physical meanings and which refer to physical events and movements. For the soul, the entire sphere of physical reality is itself *intrinsically* metaphorical. Material objects, actions and events are meant into existence in the same way that dreams and words are. Meaning matters – for matter is quite literally a materialisation of meaning, shaped by beings who mean. What we call 'soul' or 'psyche' therefore also matters, manifesting not only as Word but as Flesh. For the human body is its living dream and biological speech – its majestic material metaphor.

We misunderstand the nature of metaphor if we regard it purely as a feature of language, therefore. The word 'metaphor' is itself a covert metaphor – deriving from the Greek verb *metaphorein*: to carry or bear beyond. We misunderstand this original sense, if we regard it as one which we abstract from and then apply to language – bearing beyond the original physical and bodily senses of the words 'carry' and 'bear'. It is our incarnate, physical life which bears us beyond our native realm of soul. This life has intrinsic meaning because we ourselves, as beings, quite literally *mean things* through it, just as we do through words. All realities and all dimensions have their origin in soul – in beings who mean. But just as words can not only echo but enlarge and enrich our pre-verbal meaning and intent, so too do the languages of physical life, perception and interaction. They can enlarge our original meanings and intents and 'bear us beyond' them into new dimensions of our own being.

What we call 'speech' is not just 'verbal communication'. It includes all the ways in which, in both word and deed, look and gesture, we express ourselves and mean things to one another in physical life. Our life of speech 'bears us out' into the physical world and constitutes the fabric of our lives between birth and death. Conversely, it is our *listening life* that links us to our life of meaning – to our soul-life and to the soul-world that we inhabit between death and birth. In this world everything that we behold means something to us quite directly, without any need for representation in words or symbols. Everything we perceive 'radiates' inner meaning. It is received by the soul as meaningful speech in the same way that art is, quite independently of verbal languages.

If our lives between birth and death can be compared to stretches of speech, then the life of the soul can be compared to the intervals of silence or meditation that precede and follow these stretches. That is why a person's 'spirituality' is only indirectly linked to their life of speech – to the beliefs they espouse, the prayers or chants they utter, the symbols they cherish and the 'sacred' languages and texts they study. Its direct measure is the inward depth of their listening and the extent to which their thinking and speaking is rooted in the listening soul.

The myth of all religions of The Word – including science, linguistics and psychoanalysis – is that it is *language* (religious or scientific) that lets things be known and said. The truth of all mysticisms is that it is listening which first lets things come to presence in our awareness, whereas language merely re-presents what has already come to presence – what is already 'conscious'.

In the 'spiritual' literature of the occult and of cult movements there have been many abortive attempts to develop a 'science of soul', all of which have foundered through a lack of consideration for language itself and its relation to the listening soul. For these movements either borrowed the languages of the physical sciences to give themselves a respectable, 'modern' veneer (pseudo-science) or relied wholly on archaic languages and spiritual terminologies inherited from religious and mystical languages of the past (pseudo-religion). In both cases it was assumed that already-given religious or scientific terminologies provided a ready-made vehicle with which one could describe the soul – offering words that could be employed in the same unconscious and unquestioning manner as those we use to describe everyday objects. Today's New Age philosophers parrot the clichés that arose in the nineteenth century from this unquestioning use of language – speaking of the 'higher' spiritual 'planes' and 'vibrations' towards which mankind is evolving, or borrowing the archaic languages of Kabbalistic and Vedic mythology to posit hierarchies of spiritual consciousness and spiritual beings – Angels and Archangels, Bodhisattvas and Avatars.

All word-knowledge of the soul is itself a translation of wordless soul-experiences. The fascination exerted by the terminologies of Kabbalistic, Vedic and Buddhist philosophies is no less understandable than an interest in foreign languages and cultures per se. Every translation from a foreign language can both bring to light or abort meanings present in the original. It can also expand the inner meaning of the original, turning it into a vehicle for new and deeper revelations, new and deeper soul-senses. That is why the cultivation and development of new religions has always been linked to a work of revelatory translation. For the Vedic philosophers, Sanskrit was itself a 'foreign language' – a dead language rather like Latin, but one that was felt to be a repository of spiritual wisdom in the same way that Hebrew was for the Jews. Roman Christianity gained its particular soul-character from the use of Latin itself to translate Hebrew, Greek and Aramaic texts. Lutheranism gained its character from the use of German to translate the Bible. Buddhism flowered in China and Japan only through a long process of translating texts brought from India into Chinese, and then translating these Chinese texts into Japanese.

Understanding the importance of translation in the historical evolution of religion is one thing. Its importance in understanding the intrinsic nature of the soul is quite another. Each religion tends to see its own root language and its own spiritual terminology as a 'sacred' one, specially suited to the articulation of spiritual truth. Within the mystical traditions of each religion, however, we find recognition of the trans-linguistic nature of the soul, of its own silent and wordless speech. Spiritual terminologies borrowed from religious traditions rooted in the past cannot be simply recycled or given a modern gloss. To do so is not to bring to light but to obscure their inner meaning or 'soul-sense'. Authentic word-knowledge of the soul requires authentic soul-knowledge of the word – its role in concealing and revealing meaning. For the true 'soul of the word' is the 'word of the soul' – the wordless speech or *logos* of the *psyche*. Therefore, the deeper meaning of *psycho-logy* is 'soul-speech'.

This language of 'soul' is as much an embarrassment and scandal to current academic psychology and linguistics as Freud's sexual language was to orthodox medicine and psychiatry. Daring to speak of soul in this way – even more than daring to speak of sex, is an uncomfortable and far too open reminder of an inner knowing we all have, but few dare to admit or articulate. We come into the world naked in soul and body but very soon learn to dress the soul in camouflaging words, just as we dress the body in clothes. Using language to address and answer questions of soul directly and unashamedly, like using it to address and answer sexual questions directly, breaks our mental taboos on nakedness. Far easier to dismiss the mysteries of the soul and of language as unfathomable, and dismiss the language of soul as 'mystical'.

The words mystery, mystic, mysticism and mystical themselves are derived from the Greek word *mustai* – 'initiates'. The stem of this word is the syllable 'mu', the Greek name for the letter of the alphabet signifying the 'mmm' sound. 'Mmm' is a sound we make with the mouth closed. That is why the original Greek meaning of 'initiates' – *mustai* – meant literally 'the close-mouthed ones'. Being close-mouthed was not simply a matter of secrecy or extreme introversion. Rather it was through learning to withhold the spoken word and deepen their inward listening that the initiates re-linked themselves to the world of soul. The syllable 'mu' is also a Greek *word* – one which denotes a wordless sound – a 'groan' or 'sigh'. Groans and sighs are not merely sounds which we utter with our bodies but also sounds with which we express or 'utter' our souls in a bodily way. This is significant, for the basis of mystical psychology is the understanding that the soul utters the body and that the flesh is the living word of the soul. Just as the body utters meanings through audible sounds, thereby forming its speech, so does the soul utter the body through inaudible inner sounds or 'pre-sounds', thereby forming the flesh. The sounds of speech are an echo of those soul-sounds through which the body itself is constantly formed and re-formed. But the spoken word in turn creates a second or 'mental body' for the soul – a body of language.

The 'mystical' understanding of reincarnation is rooted in the understanding that, just as the meaning of our words lives on even when the last sounds have died on our lips, so does our soul-life continue when the body goes to sleep or gives out its last sighs. Like the breath that leaves our body in speech, ensouled with meaning, the soul that leaves our body during sleep and death is ensouled with our very being. The Greek word *psyche* meant both 'soul' and 'breath'. It referred not to the breath of the physical body alone, but to the breath which animates this body and breathes life into it, the breath of the soul. When we speak from our souls we release not only physical breath but a small portion of this soul-breath from its incarnation in physical form, giving it once again a body of meaning or 'sense'. Only someone with psychic sensibility can both listen and breathe in such a way as to absorb this soul-breath as inner meaning – as soul-sense. The experience of creative inspiration, and its energising effects on the body, has to do not with physical exercises or the intake of oxygen into the body but with this in-breath and 'in-spiration' of soul-sense. For if a person speaks with their heads and minds alone, only the outward verbal senses of their words are communicated – their words fail to provide a second body for the soul, and their soul-sense is aborted. Because of this, their soul-sense remains bound to the body and pregnant within it, communicating only through 'body language'. Similarly, if we listen with our heads and minds alone, only the outward, verbal senses of words are received, their soul-sense is left for the speaker to bear and give birth to alone. To listen with soul-sensibility, on the other hand, is truly to 'bear with' others in silence – to receive their inner meaning into the womb of our own listening souls. Only in this way can our listening help, like a midwife, to cherish and bring to fruition that which lies silently pregnant in the other person's speech.

The intensity of inward listening that characterises the inner bearing of the mystic is not a perverse introversion cutting us off from others. For it is through this inward listening that we can also establish inner listening contact with others, a contact established not with our heads or hearts alone but from our souls. People shy away from true mystics not because they are mute or uncommunicative but because even in silence we feel our souls touched by them – and this is a source of spiritual embarrassment. Ours is a society in which soul-touch and soul-intimacy is tolerated only between lovers or 'soul-mates' – or at a suitable spiritual distance created by differences or status. We have yet to learn how to overcome our spiritual embarrassment, to touch others with our souls and be touched by them in our souls. This means establishing an inner listening contact with the other person, rather than substituting for such contact with the spoken word or with physical intimacy. Ours is a society which sees only two ways of relating to others and of expressing love – speech or sex, talk or physical touch, language or love-making. That is why Freud saw sexual relations and drives – and they alone – as the 'other side' of language. Soul-science challenges this perspective, not because it is without social or individual truth, but because individuals and society themselves need to evolve to a new stage – one in which human intercourse of the soul is freed from the same type of intellectual and moral taboos that once governed sexual intercourse.

No issue reveals more dramatically the false separation of intellect and morality, 'science' and 'con-science' – and their mutual severance from questions of soul – than that of abortion. The superficiality of debate that results reflects a basic failure to recognise soul-scientific truths – the reality of the soul and its independence from the body. For to deny that the soul has a reality independent of the body is like denying that meaning has a reality independent of language and speech.

Religious anti-abortionism is based, paradoxically, upon a denial of the independent reality of the soul. For if it is the human soul which, entering the body of the embryo, foetus or new born baby, first ensouls this body with human consciousness, then the termination of pregnancy by no means implies the 'murder' of a human being. Instead the human soul simply withdraws to its own native, non-physical realm and awaits another opportunity for embodiment and incarnation – much as a speaker does when they withhold the spoken word, bide their time, and wait for a better opportunity to speak and express their meaning in words. Every abortion is anticipated by the soul concerned, for from its own perspective in the soul-world it is able to perceive likely future events in physical time. 'Soul-time' is not physical time. The soul's present is a spacious present which embraces past and future. It does so in the same way that the meaning of a speaker's utterances embraces not just the words that are presently being uttered but those that have been uttered and those as yet to be uttered.

Words that have not been spoken, like events that have not yet occurred in physical time, are not predetermined. The soul can nevertheless perceive them in the same way that the soul of a listener can anticipate words that are likely to be uttered. The listener's precognitive anticipation of what will be said arises partly from their understanding of the words already spoken and partly from sensing also what has been left unspoken. What will be said is an expression both of what has been said and what has been left unsaid. Conversely, what has been said – or left unsaid – are both an anticipation of what is yet to be said. The listener's anticipation of words that might be spoken is also based on a recollection of what the speaker has said and the words that could have been used to say it – but were not. The soul perceives events that could have happened in the same way that the soul of the listener perceives words that could have been spoken. From this point of view even an abortion that is considered but not carried out has a vivid reality for the soul, which is aware of more than one 'probable reality'. Is even the thought of abortion then, to be illegal?

Issues such as abortion mean one thing to 'pro-lifers', Catholics and their feminist opponents, and quite another to the individual human being who confronts them in real life. For the former, the questions posed are abstract ideological ones. For the latter, they are personal and concrete – not questions of good or evil, science or ethics, but questions of soul. We use words to pose questions and to formulate answers to those questions. But it is only by posing questions to our souls, giving them time to 'incubate' an answer and listening for this answer that we can make important decisions – such as whether or not to abort a pregnancy. Decision-making does not mean resolving questions with our heads or hearts alone, for these will often be in conflict, but seeding our souls with these questions and giving them time to gestate in our souls. If a pregnant woman does so she will always receive an answer in time. Sooner or later her body itself will give birth to a clear sense of what to do, generating impulses and intuitions, connecting her not only with her own soul but with the soul of the unborn child.

Just as words are translations of soul-sense, so are reasons for doing things – having or not having a baby, for example – always rationalisations of intuitions and impulses emerging from the soul. That does not mean that reason is based on groundless intuitions or irrational impulse. Rather, it is only by giving our intuitions and impulses time to incubate, and then following them, that we allow their inner rationality to emerge. By prematurely translating them into words and emotions, or acting on them without first giving them time to ripen we may interfere with this natural process. Our conscious beliefs determine which intuitions we accept and which impulses we follow. They do so through our language, which shapes how we interpret and articulate their meanings and rationalise them to ourselves. Whenever we interpret, articulate or rationalise something for ourselves in words, we 'abort' certain dimensions of meaning at the very same time as we bring others to expression. But if we use words and 'reasons' to block these intuitions and impulses we deny ourselves the opportunity to discover their inner meaning and inner rationality.

That is not to say that spontaneous, impulsive behaviour always possesses inner rationality, irrespective of how 'irrational' it seems. Whether it is so or not depends on whether it emerges from inner conflict or from inner resolution. Clear intent and 'resolve' requires time for the intuitive resolution of inner questions and inner conflict, a type of resolution that can only come about if, instead of patching up questions intellectually or emotionally, we allow ourselves to fully experience them inwardly, thereby posing them to our souls. Conflicting thoughts and feelings, together with the verbal questions they generate in our minds, are ways in which we experience the soul's inner quest to bring together separated aspects of its own being – something only the soul itself can do, not the head or heart alone.

Life questions that require us to listen to our own souls and seek answers through them are themselves not illuminated but aborted by ideologically dominated scientific or ethical debates which implicitly deny the very reality of the soul. This is true not just for the issue of abortion itself but for a whole range of social, economic, political and cultural issues. Ours is a speaking culture rather than a listening one, in which everyone is free to hold and express their own opinion on a whole variety of issues but no-one feels called upon to listen deeply to themselves or others. As a result few question the soul-less terms in which such debates are conducted, particularly in the press and media. Aborted, the soul withdraws from such shallow intellectual debates, dwelling only where the questions raised have an immediately personal significance to the human being.

The official science and consciousness of the day remains deaf to the intimate personal questions and experiences that call for soul-scientific knowledge and understanding, regarding the very idea of 'soul-science' as a hybrid and monstrous collocation. The word 'abortion' derives from the Latin *aboriri* – to die away. The deafness of official religious institutions, science and medicine results in a constant 'dying away' of the impulses and intuitions which could feed the development of soul-science. These impulses and intuitions await, like the soul, a better vehicle for their incarnation, birth and development. This vehicle is not a Messiah or cult, nor a social or scientific revolution, but a 'psychological science of language' and a 'linguistic science of the soul'.

Aspects – The Inner Alphabet of the Soul

The feeling tones and moral tones that music communicates are neither audible tones nor inaudible feelings. They are silent tones of being – 'soul-tones'. All music begins as soul-music, as an architecture of soul-tones, whether heard in the head, sensed with the heart or silently intuited. The musical language of a great composer expresses the soul-being of that individual. In the process of composition the composer alternately brings together ('com-poses') and separates out (de-composes) different 'aspects' of his own soul. Soul-tones are the wavelengths of attunement linking the composer to these soul-aspects.

If soul-tones are an inner music, then aspects are the soul's inner alphabet, the means by which soul-tones are translated *per-sonally* – 'through sound' – into faces of the self. When we make a sound we use a whole range of muscles to shape a vocal tone and give it a phonic 'shape' or 'envelope'. At the same time we give the soul-tones from which this sound arises a physical envelope and physical expression – we give it a face. A letter of the alphabet is the silent face of a sound – the way it looks on paper. Conversely, every facial expression is the silent face of a soul-sound, the way it shapes our 'look'.

Looks are more than just 'expressions'. They are ways of looking out on the world – ways of seeing. When we open our mouth wide to make an 'Aaah' sound, and at the same time imbue our facial expression with a look whose feeling tone corresponds to this sound – a look of 'wonder' or 'delight' for example – we find ourselves looking out on the world with a sense of wonder and seeing it in a new light. The tone of the 'Aaah' is now radiated through the tone of our gaze and sheds a particular light on all that we behold. Soul-tones are transformed through the look and the radiance of the eyes into 'soul-light', the 'cast' of our look. Such is the manner in which, often unbeknown to the ego, we constantly find ourselves looking out on the world through different eyes and different 'I's' – different soul-aspects.

To imbue our facial expression and look with the feeling tone of a particular sound we do not even need to make that sound audibly. The corresponding letter – the facial expression and look – is itself a sound, a 'pre-sound' or 'soul-sound' that we can hear within us even when we utter a sound silently. Aspects are both *personified* in our voice tones and radiated through looks and facial expressions – each of which constitutes a unique mask or *persona*. An individual's acquired range of vocal tones and facial expressions constitutes their *personality*. This is a blend or combination of familiar soul-aspects, united like the letters and sounds of a name, and rooted in a particular range of soul-tones. But each individual carries in their soul, and embodies in their biological genes, a huge range of other soul-tones. These constitute latent aspects of their inner soul-character which they do not normally personify in their everyday personality.

An individual's hearing is limited by the tones they themselves are capable of making. Similarly an individual's awareness of their own soul-tones, and the soul-aspects these link them to, tends to be limited to those they are capable of expressing in everyday life. Latent tones are experienced as strange feelings or inexpressible emotions, latent aspects as strange figures in their dreams. Unable to personify these aspects, individuals feel a split between their outer personality and their inner self-experience, between the feeling tones communicated by their speaking voice and the silent tones of their 'inner voice'. During schizophrenic crises the new aspects may be experienced as intrusive voices or possessing spirits. Not wanting to experience such a 'split personality', most people either repress strange feelings that come over them or seek to translate and express them in the terms of their ordinary personality. Even when the personality consciously allows itself to be transformed and possessed by these voices – as in 'trance-mediumship' or 'channelling' for example – soul-aspects are usually cloaked in the garb of spiritual 'archetypes' such as wise old Red Indians, extra-terrestrial intelligences, angelic beings, religious leaders etc. The wisdom communicated by these archetypal spirits is stereotyped 'pseudo-spiritual' wisdom that manages to say nothing fundamentally new – though they may radiate a subtle quality of feeling that is new, a meaningful 'soul-tone' that lacks only proper translation.

In normal speech we do not imbue each discrete sound in a word with its own distinct feeling tone and let it alter our entire countenance and self-experience. We skim the surface of these sounds, as in our mental-emotional life we skim the surface of our soul-aspects, merging them into a continuous stream of speech, a continuous sense of ego-identity. Were we to slow our speech down to such an extent that we allowed each speech sound to emerge from a definite soul-tone within us, letting this tone shape itself as a 'soul-sound' and as a 'soul-look' before even beginning to utter it, then we would begin to experience the true nature of our soul-being and its alphabet of aspects. Our speech would not be an egoic speech centred in the linguistic ego or 'I' but a listening speech – one that reveals the inner faces of the soul and literally *personifies* its inner richness.

In early development, the mother's resonant attunement to the infant allows her to personify shared feeling tones in her look and in the sounds and intonation patterns with which she 'coos' her baby. As soon as the infant begins to form distinct syllables, however, the mother begins to interpret these sounds, not as personifications of feeling tone but as spoken words. Gradually then, the verbal face of the child replaces its fluid musical face. Soul-tones continue to be echoed in voice and vocal intonation patterns, and speech continues to be accompanied by gestures, facial expressions and 'looks', but the child's 'alphabet' of physiognomic expression becomes limited to a particular number of letters – a restricted range of soul-aspects.

The word 'aspect' is double-sided. A 'look' is both a mode of subjective expression and also a way of seeing the objective world. Similarly, the word 'aspect' refers both to an objective face or facet of something that we perceive: a house or landscape, for example – and a particular angle of perception: the 'aspect' from which we perceive it. Soul-aspects are not merely 'parts' of the soul or sub-divisions of self. They are also windows of the soul, each of which reveals particular aspects of other people and of the world. Aspects are not only different sides of ourselves. Each is a way of both being in the world and perceiving that world, of being with others and perceiving others.

The nature and dynamics of soul-aspects transcends the division between the 'subject' and 'object' of perception. Every subjective mood or mode of perception reveals particular faces or facets of the objective world. Every aspect or facet of our experience is both a particular way of experiencing ourselves, a face of the self, and a way of experiencing something other than self, a face of the other. Aspects belong neither to 'self' nor 'other'. They are 'our-selves', plural, each a distinct, in-divisible 'letter' of our soul-alphabet. Soul-aspects are those potentials of our being which we are aware of as our root 'values' and become aware of as qualities of soul. Personality aspects are those specific qualities and values we identify with and 'personify' in ordinary life.

The ego identifies only with a particular group of soul-aspects and experiences aspects belonging to its larger alphabet as 'foreign' or 'alien' characteristics connected with other people, other cultures, other languages. The attitude of the ego is like that of a person who says: 'My name has four letters J-O-H-N – these are my letters, and all others belong to people with other names.' In doing so it denies its entire alphabet of soul-aspects, forgetting that it is in the way these letters are combined and voiced, its 'language of being' that its individuality resides – not in identification with a small group of aspects.

Our psychological 'mother tongue' in other words, is a limited range of 'letters' that we learn to identify in infancy and childhood. Our verbal 'mother tongue' on the other hand, is of course based on a complete alphabet of letters – and yet this is one alphabet, and one language among many. Languages and alphabets themselves, rather than individual letters, are the social and cultural equivalent of 'soul-letters', each with their own particular forms of pronunciation and their own indefinable soul qualities. That is why it is in the process of learning a foreign language, more perhaps than in any other sphere of learning, that we can discover new soul-aspects of our own. For at the same time as learning new sounds, letters and words we bring out new sides of our personality. Aspects, however, are not merely personality aspects or 'features', ways of speaking or acting. For just as letters are the visible *traces* of sounds so are personality aspects the visible traces of soul-aspects, 'written' in our genes and on our faces. They are the 'ways of meaning' with which we translate our 'language of being'. But the latter includes also those values or potentials of being that lie latent in our soul – its unexpressed qualities or 'soul-aspects'.

Behind a letter is a sound – a shaping or 'envelope' of vocal tone. Behind speech sounds are soul-sounds, shapings or 'envelopes' of soul-tones. Behind a voice is a physical mind and body – the speaker. Behind the inner voice of our feelings is a soul-being. Our own feelings link us to the soul-tones of our being and to the tones of our soul-being. We are the 'word' of this being, but it also has other words, other bodies, composed of similar or different 'sounds' and 'letters' – our soul-aspects. Our soul-aspects then, have a reality that transcends our own personhood, just as letters and sounds have a reality transcending any given word or name. Just as sounds shape voice tones into sounds and use them to produce articulate speech, so does our soul-being shape its 'sounds' into aspects which then leave their traces in more than one name, more than one body – more than one life. Different dimensions of psychic reality give different forms and bodies to these aspects, just as different languages give a different phonic shape or 'envelope' to vocal tones.

Every aspect of our souls has beingness – that is to say it is a being in its own right. Souls are beings who mean. The basic medium by which beings mean is tone. Our soul-being grants being to its aspects by imbuing them with its tones of being, in the same way that we grant being to our words by imbuing them with breath and voice tones. Each of us, therefore, is not merely a sum of parts, like a word with a number of letters. For each sound we utter with our voice conveys our being as a whole – transmits our voice. It also links the words we utter with other words which contain similar sounds or are uttered in a similar tone. Our personality aspects, expressed in speech and facial expression, link us like sounds and letters to countless other 'words' uttered by our soul-being – to other incarnations and personifications of the same soul-aspects.

As incarnate souls we can combine our different personality aspects, latent and expressed, in as many ways as letters can be combined to form words and names. Our 'inner name' includes all the soul-aspects we draw on over a lifetime, those we personify and those that never become personality aspects but lie latent in our character like unsounded letters. This inner name is like a word that evolves over time, dropping certain letters and adopting new ones. That is why the 'childish' game of inventing 'nonsense' words for things or creating fantasy names such as Jabberwocky for imaginary people and beings is a highly meaningful one. Every nonsense word that we create, even if we use it to name a 'thing' – an object, animal or feeling – is in fact a way of naming ourselves in a new way, bringing to expression in sound the aspects of ourselves that we find echoed in the thing we name. Foreign words and names, including sacred words, names and religious 'mantras' serve the same purpose. They have a 'ring' to them that transcends our own alphabet and lexicon, echoes latent aspects of our own souls and helps us to feel and personify these aspects. That is why foreign religious terminologies hold such an attraction. But it is above all through listening to music that we can become aware of new and unfamiliar soul-aspects with our *bodies*. Through following music with our bodies we can learn to embody these soul-aspects without naming them in words, and without translating them into already familiar emotions and personality aspects.

The emergence of different musical themes in the course of a sonata or symphony echoes the way in which different aspects of our soul-being rise into prominence within us at different stages in our lives, giving our experience a characteristic quality and tone. The combination of notes, chords and themes in musical composition, like the combinations of letters, words and phrases that form sentences, reflects the way in which we compose ourselves from groups of soul-aspects. Such combinations or 'complexes' of aspects also have beingness – they are also beings.

Represented in astrological signs, soul-aspects are hidden behind the complexes or constellations of stars in which the planets (representing personality aspects) 'move'. Together they constitute a 'music of the spheres' which does not lend itself to verbal articulation, for an astrological chart will automatically attract interpretations based on familiar mental-emotional concepts of personality aspects rather than on as yet unfamiliar feeling tones and aspects – the *unknown* planets and constellations of the soul. Represented in alphabetic signs, soul-aspects correspond to unvoiced sounds, particularly to consonants and consonantal clusters, whereas personality aspects correspond more to voice sounds and vowels. Silent vowels and voiced consonants such as 'mmm' and 'zzz' form a bridge between these two types of aspects. For consonants are shapings or 'envelopes' of unsounded soul-tones, whilst vowels are sounded, physical and vocal expressions of these tones. Silently enunciating vowels and silently voicing or 'intoning' consonants cultivates an awareness of the inner soul-sounds which find their last trace in the letters of the alphabet.

Changing a single letter in a word or name can completely alter its meaning or sound. In truth it is now a different painting, a different word, a different name. The same is true of the self. When any one aspect of our experience alters, even in a relatively minor way such as a change of mood or feeling tone, our whole being is subtly or significantly altered. The self that is feeling or doing one thing is not quite the same self that feels or does another. For every experience that the self 'has' colours its experience *of* itself. Identity and action, self and experience are not separable. In this sense Buddhism is right – there is no immutable 'self' as such. Or rather the soul is like a constantly changing symphony of its own aspects, each of which has beingness or self hood, but each of which also constantly alters and is altered by the whole.

Aspects, Listening and the Music of the Soul

Groups of letters form words, providing a vehicle for the 'incarnation' of word meanings. Groups of words provide vehicles for the incarnation of phrasal or sentence meanings; groups of sentences form paragraph meanings, textual meanings etc. Similarly, a given group of aspects provides a vehicle or body in which other, higher level soul-aspects can incarnate and dwell. We ourselves, as incarnate souls, are unique combinations of particular soul-aspects, inner faces or letters, whose combination constitute our 'inner names'. In combining and grouping our own soul-aspects we also provide a vehicle for the incarnation of other, 'deeper' or 'higher' level aspects of our own being. The aspect of our being that dreams is broader than the aspects of our being that are dreamt, for the former dreams the latter. The self that utters or writes its name has a 'broader' or 'larger' identity than the self named by that name. The identity of the self that speaks is larger than that of the self that is spoken – the latter is the person we make ourselves out to be in our words, the former the self that makes us so – and can make us otherwise by changing its words. The self that speaks is a 'being who means'. The self that is spoken is a 'being who is meant'. When we identify with our spoken selves we grant them self – being, giving them their own power to mean and speak, like a *persona* adopted by an actor. But if we reduce ourselves to our spoken selves, we become like actors who cannot throw off their 'parts'.

Our embodied soul, with its ego and personality aspects is an independent aspect of our soul-being, with its own power to mean and speak. And yet it is itself 'spoken' by higher level aspects. We contact these higher level aspects only when we withhold the spoken word ourselves and listen inwardly to the voice that speaks 'to' us within – for this is the voice of the soul-aspects that 'speaks' us.

There are, however, 'alternate selves' which remain unknown to us because they combine our own aspects in different ways or in combinations with other unfamiliar aspects. These may be incarnate in other places in the current world or in other historical epochs, or both. At the same time their characteristics lie latent in our genes and in our root values. Past and future selves, like past and future lives, combine and express our soul-aspects in different ways. Each lives not only in our memory or anticipation but in its own present. In soul-time these past and future selves each have their own range of possible futures – and pasts – creating a multiplicity of selves following time-lines in parallel universes. The larger life of the soul can only be understood by comparing it with a book written in countless different versions. Every revision of the book alters the character of the book as a whole. Sentences, paragraphs or chapters written later may lead the author to revise earlier ones. The revision of earlier sentences, paragraphs or chapters may lead in turn to the revision of later ones. But the original drafts of each sentence, paragraph or chapter retain their life as parts of other 'alternate' books.

Every word, paragraph and chapter written by an author has repercussions on a book as a whole, lending it a tone which puts it in greater or lesser kinship with alternate 'incarnations' of the book as a whole. When we close our 'book of life' we may begin preparing a new book ('reincarnation'). Alternatively we may concentrate first on revising an old one in specific ways (retrocarnation), or instead of reincarnating explore a particular life in as wide as possible a range of different versions ('trans-carnation'). But the very process of living a given life involves reincarnation, retrocarnation and trans-carnation. Every decision we take and everything we experience in our personal reality links us to alternate lives and alternate selves, past, present and future. We identify with certain aspects rather than others, just as the author identifies with certain wordings rather than others. Before, during and after he writes, the author listens – exploring different possible wordings. But in identifying with a particular wording, the book as a whole is changed – and so is the author. Every life-decision, major or minor is not just an act of mind or body. It is an 'act of spirit', for it involves an identification with certain soul-aspects or groups of aspects. Acts of identification are not acts of doing but acts of being – for by their very nature they alter the very identity of the agent. Ego-identity on the other hand, is the illusion that there is a part of us that remains unchanged by our own decisions and experiences, a subject immune from its verbs and complements. Yet for every ego there is an 'alter ego' – a self that chooses differently and that follows a different but parallel time line. The self that feels, says or does one thing is not quite the same self as the self that feels, says or does another, but the word 'I', the linguistic mirror of the ego, enables it to regard all its feelings, statements and actions as part of its 'own' continuous identity.

The ego is an aspect of the embodied soul, but one whose nature it is to regard itself as separate from all others. Its function is to act as an intermediary between the soul and the physical world – to represent the soul in the world and report the world to the soul. And yet through the word 'I' the ego seeks to maintain a firm boundary between *what* we feel, say and do and *who* we think and feel ourselves to *be*. The ego is the guardian between the what and the who, ensuring that our thoughts and feelings, words and deeds, do not alter our sense of who we are. As egos we regard thoughts and feelings as private property, even talking of our souls and bodies as something we 'have'. This helps us to feel that we are in full 'possession' of ourselves. If what we think or feel begins to alter our sense of who we are, we may partially or wholly lose our sense of self-possession and instead feel 'not quite ourselves'. Indeed we may even feel possessed by an alien identity.

Experiencing ourselves from the perspective of new and unfamiliar soul-aspects can easily be experienced and interpreted as a state of 'possession'. But were we to *fully* identify with new and different aspects of the soul we would not experience this as possession at all, nor even lose our identity – for each soul-aspect, being part of the whole, also links us to other aspects and contains the whole within it. The problem is that the ego, by its very nature, is incapable of acts of identification, for these, by definition, alter the identity of the agent. Ego-acts are acts of doing, carried out by an agent that is separate from and unaltered by its 'own'. Acts of identification are acts of being – acts through which the soul grows and transforms itself. Through identification we do not lose our identities. Instead we link ourselves to other aspects of our own soul-being, and to our broader and deeper identity – our soul-identity. Ego-identity itself rides on and depends on this larger soul identity. Our identification *of* different parts of the 'self' and 'other' using words and language would mean nothing without a certain capacity to identify *with* those parts – thereby experiencing 'other selves'.

The ego is the verbal face of the soul, represented by the immutable subject pronoun 'I' and counter-posed to a 'you' or an 'it'. The soul is the autistic and artistic core of the self – its musical core – whose every mood is not only a different way of experiencing the self but a different way of experiencing other people and the world. It is *autistic* because any attempt to use the word 'I' to describe a change in ourselves or in our experience of the world implicitly denies that change as a change in our *selves* or in our *self*-experience. As soon as 'I-talk' begins we identify once again with our egos and with a particular way of seeing and being in the world based on the language mind – the division of reality into subject, verb and object.

Acts of perception are not essentially acts of an ego or subject but the expression of an inter-action between perceiver and perceived – one which alters both perceiver and perceived, and reveals new aspects of both. The language mind, on the other hand, *translates* this perceptual interaction into something going on 'in' the perceiver or in the perceived, 'in' me or 'in' you – something either purely subjective, purely objective or purely the act of the subject on an object.

The division of language into subjects, verbs and objects itself imposes a particular structure on our perception of reality, reinforcing our ego-identity, and separating it from the 'musical' intercourse of soul that links one being with another through their ways of meaning (their personality aspects) and the moods of soul which generate them (their soul-tones and soul-aspects). This intercourse is like the interaction that goes on between members of an orchestra as they play, for it is an interaction that is indeed essentially *musical* rather than verbal – an interaction of soul rather than one based on separated 'subjects' and 'objects'. A conductor's gestures or a musician's playing do not express or create the music. Their body language is an inner *response* to the music, revealing their way of listening to and hearing this music. The music as such is not the sounds made by the orchestra, nor even the composer's score. For the latter, too, is a response to something that the composer feels and hears in his own soul – to its music. Similarly an individual's body-speech does not 'communicate' their soul-tones, or soul-music or soul-aspects. Like the body language of a musician or conductor it is a response to this music, their way of meaning and playing it to us. It translates soul-aspects into personality aspects. Soul-aspects as such are embodied only in stillness and silence – only in the intervals and pauses of both speech, movement and music.

Our soul-being as a whole can be compared to the soul of a great composer, expressed through an ever changing symphony of soul-aspects. Its incarnations can be compared to orchestras or ensembles of personality aspects which each play this music in their own way. The body can be compared to the musical instrument, a resonant chamber in which soul-tones resound and are also translated into audible tones. Each personality aspect – each musician – in the ensemble of personality contributes its own tone and tune to a performance, plays it own part expressing the music of the soul. The ego can be compared to the conductor of the orchestra, who keeps track of all its sections, and gives direction to individual musicians. In order to do this properly, the conductor must also listen inwardly and attune to the soul of the music that is being played – to the soul-being of the composer. Similarly, in order to do its job properly, the ordinary personality must develop an inner ego that is attuned to its own soul-music, able to re-link its ensemble of personality aspects with the soul-aspects they arise from, whilst at the same time finding ways of letting as yet unexpressed soul-tones and soul-aspects sound through. The 'outer ego' is the verbal and egoistic face of the conductor, his speaking self that speaks itself through the word 'I'. The 'inner ego' is the inward looking musical 'eye' of the personality – the inward listening self that attunes itself to the soul of the music and the music of the soul.

Whether we listen to a piece of music properly depends on our capacity to play along with the music in our souls, to associate it with aspects of ourselves we know from everyday life, whilst at the same time linking these personality aspects with the basic soul-tones from which they arise. If we do so the music will link us to our source aspects – our soul-aspects – letting us look out through their eyes. The composition we are listening to will literally 're-compose' our own personality-aspects and allow new soul-aspects to shine through.

Using music to hear our own souls speak is only possible if we adjust ourselves to the type of listening which the music itself arises from. Music is composed by a process of inward listening and echoes the depth and character of this listening as well as the 'personality' of the composer. Different types of music demand different types of listening because they are born from different types of listening. To listen to a piece of music being performed is therefore paradoxical for it involves listening to several ways of listening – to the composer's listening, the conductor's listening, the musicians' listening. This is less impossible than it may seem, for whenever we listen to a person speak we are also listening to the way they are listening to themselves and others. We know when a person's words are a *listening response* from their souls, or whether they are simply 'rabbiting on', 'sounding off' or talking 'off the top of their head'.

When musicians play together, they are of course also listening to one another. The soul-contact they have with each other is established not with their outer egos but with their inner egos – their listening selves. Through listening to music we can hear our souls echoed in sound. But listening to music is also a way of learning to make inner listening contact with other people through the inner music of our feeling tones, and the 'soul-speech' that issues from them. This is the type of contact I call 'inner voice communication'.

Other people's words and way of speaking, like foreign languages, only begin to mean something to us personally when we appreciate the difference in the way they 'put things'. Simply to understand the given meaning of a person's words or what they refer to is not enough. It is the difference in their way of putting and saying things – of meaning them – that means something. 'Ways of meaning', of course, include 'body-speech' as well as words. Here again, however, it is not the fact that we can understand what is 'communicated' through body language that makes it personally meaningful. Nor is personal meaning a result of us 'projecting' some meaning onto a person's body language anymore than it is a result of projecting some meaning into their words. So-called 'projections' are a defence against acknowledging the *intrinsic* meaning that another person's way of expressing themselves has for us – its difference to our own.

Every significant 'other' in our lives personifies, for us, a different way of expressing and bearing forth our own soul-aspects, a different way of translating our own 'language of being' into 'ways of meaning' – into voice and body-speech. Conversely, every significant other also characterises for us a different inner bearing, a different way of dwelling within ourselves and embodying particular soul-aspects in silence and stillness.

Every significant relationship is a mutual relation in which both partners personify and embody each other's soul-aspects in a way which is meaningfully different – not only 'mirroring' each other's aspects but bearing them back to the other, transformed and translated into a different language of being and a different way of meaning. Another person's way of expressing themselves through voice and gestural body-speech is intrinsically meaningful not because of what it communicates but because, consciously or unconsciously, it suggests to us a different way of expressing ourselves – a different way of personifying our own soul-aspects. Conversely, another person's characteristic 'inner bearing' means something to us because it shows us a way of 'bodying our souls' and 'ensouling our words' in stillness and inner silence. For soul aspects can be communicated *without* needing to express them in vocal tones and gestural body-speech – without needing to translate them into personality aspects.

Personality aspects communicate in speech through the physical body and physical self-expression. In doing so, they indirectly give expression to soul-aspects and a person's soul-character – their way of listening to themselves. But soul-aspects can also communicate directly – from soul to soul. They do so through the listening body and its inner voice – the soul-body and the soul-voice. Listening is an 'inner voice communication' – an active modulation of the silent undertones of our listening.

Our listening, too, sets a tone, not a voiced tone but a silent tone modulated by the inner voice. It is through the silent tones of our listening, of this inner voice, that we establish a particular 'wavelength' of relation to ourselves and others. We attune, through these wavelengths, to particular soul-aspects of our own, receiving each other's speech on the 'frequency band' of these aspects and attracting meanings which can ride on them.

Individuals alive at the same time and sharing the same physical spaces seem to share a common physical world, just as they may seem to share a common language. In fact, just as each of us gives a different colouration to the senses of words, even though they form part of a common language, so does each of us experience the common world of the senses in a different way. The illusion of a common world is shaped by the illusion of a common language. Without common perceptions and shared word meanings we cannot conceive the possibility of contact and communication with others. In truth, we understand each other's souls not because a given word – or perceptual object – means the same thing to everyone, but precisely because it does not. Common words and worlds are a medium for the communication and evolution of differences in our individual ways of seeing and understanding things – soul-differences which are expressed in our differing experience of the physical world.

We have not begun to understand the magnitude of these individual differences, restrained by the fear that if we did so, the illusion of a common world would dissolve, and we would instead discover the totally alien character, not only of each other's souls, but of each other's worlds. The understanding that it is such differences that give *meaning* to this common world, and to 'value' the difference we perceive in others, is not merely to 'respect' or 'understand' this difference. It is to find something of value in it for oneself – to let it make a difference to us and change us, to let it mean something to us and value this meaning. That is why the fact that we have 'understood' or 'respected' someone's words by no means guarantees that we value them – that we have let them work on us and mean something to us. The way we listen, and the extent to which, in listening, we truly heed and value soul-differences has a central role in shaping what is called our destiny or 'karma'. We totally misinterpret the 'karmic law' if we understand it as a sort of judicial punishment visited on us in this life for sins committed in a past life.

The understanding of 'destiny' or 'karma' is not rooted in a single 'law' or 'principle', but on a soul-scientific understanding of communication, relating and individual value-fulfilment. Value fulfilment comes about not only through acknowledging a commonality of 'shared values' but also through valuing differences in the expression of these values. This means finding value in these differences for oneself, letting them make a difference and allowing oneself to be changed by the difference of others. To reject or maltreat another individual or group because of differences in their personal, sexual, racial, political or cultural values makes no more sense than to reject or maltreat them because they use different words or a different language. It is not wrong because it is 'politically incorrect', or a denial or 'universal' values. It is wrong because in rejecting particular values we in fact deny that these are values at all – for values are by nature particularities – expressions of difference – that can be valued by all.

The so-called 'law of karma' must be understood not as a judicial law but as a law which expresses the very nature of the soul, its multiple inner aspects and values. It can be translated as follows: values and soul-aspects that you do not acknowledge as voices in yourself will invariably be expressed by other people you know. Conversely, voices and values you reject in you will, sooner or later (in this life or the next) come to be experienced for what they are – your own inner voices and values. However strongly you disagree with someone's words or disapprove of their deeds therefore, to heed them in accordance with 'karma' is to recognise them as an echo of latent values and voices of your own.

We do not listen because another person speaks. The way another person speaks, and the sides of themselves they show us, is itself a response to the way we are listening to them; just as the way we speak to others, and the sides of ourselves that we show to them, is a response to the way we are listened to. When we listen, it is as if we draw each other's planets (personality aspects) into the field of our own astrological constellations (soul-aspects). Conversely, whenever we speak, our own personality aspects are drawn into the field of each other's soul-aspects and become vehicles for the expression of the latter. When we speak we do not only express ourselves, for we also function as conscious or unconscious mediums or 'channels' for each other's soul-aspects

The Soul-Body and the Body-Soul

Rudolf Steiner described speech as 'invisible gesture' and gesture as 'visible speech'. This was the basis of Eurythmy, a movement art based on gestures which articulates in a silent, bodily way the vowels and consonants of speech. The English word 'gesture' echoes the verb 'gestate', just as its German equivalent (*Gebärde*) is closely related to the verb *Gebären* (to bear) and also *Gebärden* – to bear or comport oneself in a particular way. If what we call 'character' is the way we bear our souls silently within us, and 'personality' is the way we bear them forth through sound (*per-sonare*), then the relation of character and personality can be seen as a relation between the inner bearing or comportment of an individual and the physical and vocal gestures that then emerge or are borne forth from this bearing.

Speech and song are both forms of vocal gesture and may at the same time be accompanied by bodily gestures. But it is in the inward listening that precedes speech or song that we establish the inner bearing from which these gestures arise – an inner bearing expressed in our physical posture, comportment and countenance. That is why, before she gives voice to a single note, the trained singer first listens inwardly to compose herself and find her inner voice – the inner bearing and outer comportment whose 'soul-mood' or 'soul-tone' corresponds to that of the song. As she sings, every modulation of her inner tone and bearing finds expression in the particular vowels and consonants she voices. These form the words of the song, whose inner meaning can communicate only if the inner tone and bearing of the singer's soul within her body – her soul-tone and soul-bearing – is one that allows her to bear this soul-meaning forth in her vocal tones and gestures.

Our soul-bearing, at any given time, has to do with the way we dwell as souls within our bodies, and the way in which we experience our inwardly sensed bodies as a 'soul-body'. Just as the body can be seen as the womb of the soul, so can a particular soul-bearing be compared to a position or bearing of the foetus within the womb that bears it, or alternatively with a position of the earth in relation to the womb of the heavens. Getting our bearings in a situation is a process of feeling around in ourselves, and establishing a central locus or 'coordinate point' of awareness from which to relate to what is going on in and around us. Through our inner bearing we adopt a particular inner relation to all of our soul-aspects, known and unknown.

If inner soul-aspects are projected outwards, they are perceived as external signs – as omens or star signs, for example. Then, it is the position of the earth in relation to the sun, planets and cosmic constellations that becomes a symbol of the soul's inner bearing in relation to its aspects, and a way of 'reading' the soul. Just as it is our inner soul-bearing that prefigures our words and deeds, so also were the positions of the stars read as a prefigurement of actual events on earth, events which were understood as the speech of the gods. With the development of writing, language and the internal sphere of the mind gradually replaced the spheres of the heavens as the principal medium in which soul-experience was inscribed and read. Letters, originally pictograms of the world or of the constellations, were linked with speech sounds, shapings of the mouth and positions of the tongue within the oral cavity.

The word 'infant' derives from the Latin *in-fans* – non-speaking. Sounds do not yet have verbal senses, and yet for the infant the oral cavity is a microcosm of the body-soul. For it is in learning to distinguish its own sounds from those of its sonorous field or environment, that the infant begins, at the same time, to experience its soul as something bounded by a more or less permeable sonorous envelope or body. The sounds the infant makes with its body are shapes or envelopes of audible tones. At the same time they echo inner sounds – the shaping of feeling tone within its own resonant soul. It is through resonance between the shape and tone of its audible sounds and these inner sounds that the infant shapes its own inner sense of bodyhood.

Every speech sound has an inner bodily sense for the infant – shaping the felt substantiality, tone and texture of its inwardly sensed body or soul-body. In making the 'm' sound, for example, the baby experiences the sensed interiority of its body as a womb-like space, permeated by an inner soul warmth with its own fluid substantiality. In making a stop sound such as a 'b' sound, on the other hand, the infant feels its own surface boundedness as a body. For, in firmly bounding its own oral cavity by sealing its lips, the infant feels its body, as a whole, as a *balloon*-like membrane filled with the psychical *breath* of its own self-awareness.

Of course, the infant explores many different ways of physically producing a 'b' sound – whilst *dribbling* for example. In doing so it experiences the relation between its own bodily sense of the insideness and outsideness to the boundary it shapes with the 'b'. The verbal senses of many words containing the 'b' sound (*boundary, barrier, border, membrane, bubble, balloon, burst, break, blurt, dribble, embarrass* etc.) bear witness to its felt bodily sense – not least the word *body*. Different sub-groups of verbs containing the 'b' sound each express a different relationship of the soul to its own felt bodily boundaries – *abiding* within them, challenging them (*barrage, battle*), overstepping them (*blush, embarrass*). Whether such 'b-words' refer to bodily acts such as *burping*, vocal acts like *bellowing*, speech acts such as *boasting*, or purely 'inward' acts such as *brooding*, they all echo the basic 'physio-logical' meaning of the 'b' sound. All speech sounds are used in specific ways by the infant soul, not to utter words but to utter and experience its own bodyhood in specific ways – to shape its body-soul.

The reason why many *meditational mantras* such as OM, HUM and MU contain the 'm' sound is that, in making this sound we not only seal our lips, but recreate a sense of dwelling as beings within a comforting womb-like *warmth body*. This bodily sense of the 'm' sound is also echoed in the verbal senses of words such as *warmth, womb, amnion, membrane, memory, medium, meditation.*

Individual speech sounds do not 'have' meanings in the same way that words do. Instead they *embody* meaning. The root meaning of the word *mantra* is liberation (*tra*) of mind and meaning (*man*). Mantras are sounds whose inner resonances influence the felt shape of, and tone, our inwardly sensed body. Meditation is the inward expansion of the resonant inner soul-space of our bodies, reconnecting us to our own soul-body. The body of a word is its sound. The soul of a word its sense. But the mantric meaning of a word has to do with the *inner sense* of each of its *sounds* as such, a sense that has essentially to do with our own inwardly sensed body and its resonant inner soul-space. Together these constitute a distinct inner soul-body. The liberation of meaning or sense from the word, through mantra meditation, was understood as a *yog*a or 'discipline' by which we could reawaken our sense of a larger, shape-shifting soul-body, transcending the confines or 'yoke' of its physical boundaries.

Our larger soul-body can compared to a balloon, the incarnate portion of our souls to a part of this balloon into which we have pressed a finger. The sensed boundary of our bodies in physical space can be compared to the surface of the balloon skin surrounding this finger. Our perception of physical space around us, and other bodies within that space, can be compared to our finger's perception of the space *within* the balloon and its perception of other fingers that may be pressed into it. The inner surface of the balloon, as perceived by our finger and other fingers pressed into it, is comparable to the perceived horizon of cosmic space. The space around the balloon, on the other hand, is analogous to what lies beyond the boundaries of physical space as we perceive it from within the balloon. The inner space of the balloon is the cosmos as each individual perceives it within their own balloon-like sphere of awareness. The outer surface of this sphere is aptly called the 'astral' body, being open to what lies beyond the starry heavens as we perceive them from within the balloon. The astral body is surrounded by an *unbounded* soul-space of awareness, albeit one which is layered like an onion – consisting of 'spiritual' skins or balloons which constitute the different *spheres* of the soul world.

The balloon itself is a boundary or skin between the space within and around it, skin being the root meaning of the Greek word for flesh (*sarx*). The fleshly substantiality of our bodies, like the material substantiality of other bodies in space, is a skin or boundary. But just as the flesh of the balloon is made of atoms and molecules, so our own flesh is composed of units of atomic, molecular and cellular awareness – each of which can be compared to a micro-balloon. Together, these units of awareness, or 'micro-balloons', make up both the fleshly skin of our soul 'fingers' and the fleshly fabric, or world skin, of the material world around them. Our *body-soul* is the aware inwardness of the atoms, molecules and cells that constitute the fleshly skin of our souls, their collective consciousness.

Our body-soul takes shape in the womb of the mother's flesh, and thus of her own body-soul. The incarnating soul does not, at first, dwell within the embryonic or foetal body alone but in the womb sphere as a whole. The initial fleshly boundary or membrane of the foetal soul-body is the amniotic sac. The initial boundary of its body-soul, on the other hand, is the meninges. The waters within the amnion are a fluid medium, transmitting sounds from within and beyond the mother's body. The womb itself is a fleshly metaphor of the resonant soul, the amnion being its bodily shape or boundary. But the incarnating soul itself remains unbounded by its fleshly, maternal womb. Its only boundary is the womb of its own larger soul-body, comparable to a balloon. Incarnation is the involution or infolding of a part of this balloon's surface, comparable to the vaginal shape that results from a phallic like finger pressing into a balloon. This is reflected in the way the fleshly skin, or body-soul, of the foetal soul-body – the meninges – intrudes from the amniotic sac. After the waters break and the umbilical cord is cut, a spiritual *amnesia* slowly begins to set in (Greek *mnesis* – 'remembrance'). Having left its mother's womb, the baby continues to dwell within the womb of its own fleshly body-soul, which remains intimately connected to that of the mother. As it sleeps, however, the baby's awareness returns to its spiritual soul – the larger soul-space surrounding its own balloon-like soul-body. Only gradually does it develop, whilst awake, a sense of the involuting finger-shaped portion of this balloon – the inner soul-space of its own fleshly body. Only gradually does the sensory surface of this finger become awake to the outer 'physical' space of awareness around it, a space paradoxically enclosed by the inner surface of its own larger soul-body.

The foetus can sense, from sounds resonating in the womb, that beyond her flesh lies an entire physical world of other human beings. Similarly, human beings once sense that beyond the womb of the heavens lay an entire soul world of spiritual beings. They recognised cosmic bodies such as stars and planets as the embodiment of these spiritual beings, and saw, in the concentric spheres of the planets, a reflection of concentric spheres of awareness that constitute the world of soul and spirit. Today, this world and its beings is conceived in purely materialistic terms, as a world of outer space and extra-terrestrial beings.

The German word for the womb or uterus is *Mutterleib* or 'mother body'. Our soul-body is our true mother body, symbolised both by the maternal womb, the womb of cosmic space and those 'mother ships' with which aliens visit us, and into which they supposedly abduct us. It is interesting how these 'aliens' are perceived as having bodies which, with their large eyes and heads and fragile limbs, bear a marked resemblance to the foetal body. That is not to say that UFO sightings, or experiences of alien abduction, are simply metaphors of pre-natal experiences in the womb that bore the person; that 'good' and 'bad' aliens are merely symbols of the 'good' compassionate mother or the 'bad' invasive or engulfing mother, or that their probing clinical instruments are memories of a clinicalised hospital birth, or of intrusive mothers and abusive fathers. The imagery certainly suggests this *psychoanalytic* interpretation of UFOs as Utero-Foetal-Objects. But given that the womb is itself a fleshly symbol of our soul-body, and of the larger soul world surrounding it, it may be that the all-too-human imagery of UFOs represents our own human *perceptual* interpretation of something quite different – not an intrusion of physical beings from other *planets* but of spiritual beings from other *planes* or *spheres* of awareness. This intrusion appears to occur in space – but what is 'space' except the three-dimensional sphere of our own spatial *awareness* as human beings?

The saucer-shaped, oblong, spherical or *shape-shifting* form of UFOs may not be a perception of physical space vehicles, but an external perceptual interpretation of soul vehicles – the encapsulated or shape-shifting soul-bodies of beings travelling through soul-space. The lights, sounds and tingling sensations that accompany the manifestation of these visitors from the stars, may be a somatic experience of the 'contact' they make with the surface skin of our own soul vehicle – our own 'astral' body.

An ancient knowing or *gnosis* understood that we ourselves are aliens; we ourselves are visitors to the physical plane, and sphere of awareness, that we perceive as our planet and the outer space surrounding it. That were we to perceive the shifting shape of each other's inner soul bodies, we would be shocked at the variety of human and non-human forms they can take, whether animal or alien. That we ourselves have broken through the spiritual spheres of awareness that surround this sphere. Today however, human beings have become alienated from their own inner being, the part of us that is forever unborn and already dead, for it has never ceased to abide within the world of soul and spirit from whence we came. That is why it is not from modern Hollywood science fiction cinema, but ancient Mandaean scriptures that the word 'Alien' first gained its significance.

In the name of the first great Alien life from the worlds of light, the sublime that stands above all works.

In the name of that Alien man who forced his way through the worlds, came, split the firmament and revealed himself.

Manda means knowledge – *gnosis*. According to the Mandaean tradition, we are still called by that other, forgotten 'alien' self that constitutes our innermost being. Not called from the distances of outer space but called from the distances of inner space that surround it: "He stands at the outer rim of the world and calls to the elect." Those that help human beings to hear this call of this Forgotten One, our inner being, were known as the *Uthra*. For 'UFO', we can read something entirely different: *Uthras of the Forgotten One.*

Daoist wisdom too, acknowledged an inner self and an inner body that remains unborn and undeveloped: the *golden embryo* whose abode is the abdominal womb space of the soul, the *hara*.

SOUL-SPACE
AND
THE SOUL-BODY

Coordinate Points
of the Inner Cosmos

S cience understands the human body as a physical organism
bounded by its own skin, a self-enclosed consciousness or
'subject' looking out at a world of 'objects' in space. People
have lost any sense that the apparently 'empty' space around them is
part of their own larger spatial *sphere of awareness* – that their
awareness, far from being bounded by their bodies, actually
permeates and fills the space around them in the same way that air
does, surrounding other bodies in space. Similarly, they have lost any
sense that what they experience as the boundary of their own body is
merely a localised spatial configuration of a larger *body of awareness*
– a body with its own *unbounded* spatiality. Head, heart and hara are
inner 'centres' of this spatially unbounded body or *soul-body*. They
are also 'coordinate points' of its outer and inner spheres of spatial
awareness. Together these constitute a bodily *soul-space* that knows
no inner or outer boundaries. This bodily soul-space is not merely a
'mind space' enclosed within our heads, nor is it bounded by the
dimensions of our physical body. For as Heidegger points out:

> When I direct someone towards a windowsill with a gesture of my
> right hand, my bodily existence as a human being does not end at the
> tip of my index finger. While perceiving the windowsill…. I extend
> myself bodily far beyond this fingertip to that windowsill. In fact,
> bodily I reach out even further than this to touch all the phenomena,
> present or merely visualized, represented ones.

When I go toward the door of the lecture hall, I am already there, and I could not go to it at all if I were not such that I am there. I am never here only, as this encapsulated body; rather, I am there, that is, I already pervade the room, and only thus can I go through it.

Soul-space has qualitative rather than quantitative dimensions and boundaries. What we sense inwardly as our own bodies is nothing more than the inwardly sensed boundary, shape and substantiality of the qualitative *soul-space* we find ourselves in as human beings. The root meaning of the verb 'to be' is 'to dwell'. Qualitative soul-space is nothing abstract or esoteric. It is the essential space in which we dwell and move. We experience it in all sorts of ways so familiar to us that we take them for granted:

When we feel a closeness or distance to others that has nothing to do with our physical distance from them.

When we feel the bodily boundaries between ourselves and another person inwardly 'melting' or 'stiffening'.

When we feel ourselves creating a protective force field around us that wards others off.

When we feel a complete loss of boundaries, as if our 'shields are down' and we are vulnerably exposed to an environment in which the slightest thing can get 'under our skin'.

When our bodies feel inwardly 'out of shape' or 'twisted.'

When we feel 'elevated', 'high' or 'floating on cloud nine' or 'heavy', 'down' and 'sunk' in depression.

When we feel ourselves exploding or imploding, 'fragmented' or 'in form', 'all over the place' or 'together'.

When we feel 'spaced out' or 'beside' ourselves, bodiless or out of our bodies.

When we feel someone's gaze 'penetrating' to the core of our being, or feel as if we are peering into their souls.

When we feel 'drawn out' of ourselves and merged with our surroundings – whether a city or natural landscape, a political or sporting event, a social event or cultural environment.

When we feel 'imbalanced' even though our feet stand firmly on the ground.

When we feel that we have 'lost our bearings' or 'lost our balance'.

When we feel ourselves inwardly 'expanding' or 'contracting', 'reaching out' to someone or 'shrinking away' from them.

Lakoff and Johnson regard this sort of language as *metaphorical* – and have recognised that *language is permeated by spatial-corporeal metaphors* of this sort. Thus we talk of being in a good or bad 'space', of feeling 'high' or 'low', of approaching things from a different 'angle', 'moving on' in our lives, 'living it up', or 'being let down'. We talk of what is going on 'in' someone or what they 'let out'. We talk of people withdrawing 'into' or coming 'out of' their own shells, 'spacing out', feeling 'uplifted' by good news or 'carried away' by their emotions.

But if such language is simply metaphor, what exactly is it a metaphor of? Many spatial-corporeal metaphors seem to be metaphors of emotional states. But the very word 'emotion' is itself a spatial-corporeal metaphor: 'e-motion' or 'outward motion'. Similarly many of the words we use to name specific emotions are also spatial metaphors. The words 'anguish', 'anger' and 'anxiety', for example, all have a root *spatial* meaning of 'narrowness' or 'narrowing'. Lakoff and Johnson 'point out' – another metaphor – that intellectual discourse is no less dominated by metaphor than emotional language. Thus we talk of 'putting forward', 'sticking to' or 'tearing down' an argument, thesis or proposition. Even apparently abstract terms such as 'intellect', 'logic' and 'metaphor' itself have their roots in words referring to spatial-corporeal movements. The word 'abstract' derives from Latin *ab-strahere*, to 'lift off'. The word 'metaphor' itself derives from the Greek verb *metaphorein* – to 'carry across'. The words 'intellect' and 'logic' derive from the Greek *legein* – to gather and lay out. And as we have seen, the language of physics is not exempt from metaphor, the very word 'physics' arises from the Greek verb *phuein* – to emerge or arise.

What Lakoff and Johnson conclude is that *all* language, whether poetic or prosaic, emotional or intellectual, symbolic and scientific has a metaphorical character, consisting as it does, of spatial-corporeal metaphors based on the complementary spatial polarities of *up and down, forward and back, left and right, in and out. Soul science* challenges this conclusion – literally and metaphorically 'revolving' or overturning it. For what Lakoff and Johnson are saying is that when, for example, we speak of feeling *close* to someone, this is a 'metaphor' rooted in spatial-corporeal experience. Soul science turns this conclusion on its head, arguing that we move closer to people in a bodily way because, in this way, we can embody an already felt-sense of inward closeness to them. The space of this inner closeness, however, is not a measurable quantitative space but soul-space – an immeasurable *qualitative space of awareness.*

Spatial-corporeal experience, therefore, far from being the basis of linguistic metaphor is *itself a 'metaphor'* of experience in qualitative soul-space. Corporeal *motions and emotions* give metaphorical expression to *motions of awareness* in a soul-space. When we go from feeling 'low' to 'feeling high' our emotions themselves give expression to *real* motions in a qualitative soul-space of awareness – a motion from one spatial quality of awareness to another. The language with which we express such motions is not merely metaphorical but a literal reference to such inner motions of awareness.

When we experience ourselves as 'distant' or 'close' to someone, 'open' or 'closed off', we are referring quite literally to experienced spatial qualities of our own *body of awareness*. When we talk of being in a good or bad 'space' we are not referring literally to the physical space around us, nor are we merely speaking metaphorically. We are referring quite *literally* to the *qualitative space* we find ourselves in and the specific qualities of awareness that characterise that space. When we then find ourselves in another 'better' space, this is not because we have necessarily moved our bodies to some other location. Instead we have experienced a *motion* in this qualitative space – a movement from one quality of awareness to another. We experience this motion not only as an e-motional change we are aware of 'in' our bodies, but as a change in the *whole quality of our bodily awareness* – a change from one *bodily* tone and texture of awareness to another. When we feel ourselves moving inwardly 'closer' to others or 'distancing' ourselves from them, 'going into' or 'coming out of our shells', or just when we feel ourselves 'uplifted' or 'carried away', we are not, in the first place, describing corporeal movements in extensional space but movements of awareness in a qualitative space with its own *intrinsic* bodily dimensions. Lakoff and Johnson's whole view of language is distorted by the old materialistic assumption that basic reality consists of extensional bodies in an objective physical space. But the essential body we inhabit as beings is our own soul-body or body of awareness. This is a body which has its own intrinsic spatial dimensions; that inhabits and shapes its own qualitative space of awareness or soul-space. In contrast to the materialistic linguistics of Lakoff and Johnson, which roots language in spatial-corporeal experience, soul science understands spatial-corporeal motion as the *embodiment* of motion in qualitative space – its transposition into spatio-temporal movement. It understands 'emotion' as the felt bodily *experience* of motion in qualitative space, with specific emotions giving expression to specific directions of motion in qualitative space. It understands dreaming as the dramatised *expression* of such motions in qualitative space – specific dream locations being symbols of different coordinate points of awareness in that space.

Lakoff and Johnson have observed correctly that there is also a covert *moral* dimension to spatial-corporeal metaphor. Over most of human history, prejudice has dictated that certain spatial *poles* of qualitative space are 'good' and others 'bad'. Thus theologians of all faiths and persuasions have spoken of man's 'higher' and 'lower' nature, and even today the ideology of New Age spirituality favours 'higher' frequency spiritual vibrations over 'lower ones'. Modernist ideologies, on the other hand, have contrasted the 'forward' march of technological progress with 'backward looking' or conservative traditions. Phrases such as 'things are looking up', 'taking a step forward' or 'getting out of difficulty' reveal the way in which *upward, forward* and *outward* motions are valued more highly than *downward, backward* or *inward* ones. Thus we go 'up' to heaven, but down into hell.

Children are still taught at school that coordinate points in space are defined by qualitatively undifferentiated axes. Our own *bodies* tell us that these axes are qualitatively distinct from one other, and that these qualitative distinctions have to do with qualities of awareness. In contrast to animals we are vertical beings. We sit, stand and wake 'up', yet we lie *down* horizontally to 'fall' asleep. The body-space of the human is not uniform and undifferentiated nor are its dimensions of movement. The movements of lying down and standing up, moving forward and backward, spreading ourselves out sideways or stiffening like a pole, each embody or evoke quite different qualities of awareness. Dance is an unceasing exploration of the infinite qualitative dimensions belonging to the 'three dimensions' of body-space.

Unlike basic school geometry, both language and our lived experience of space recognise that there are, in fact, not three but *four* basic dimensions of space. The fourth dimension of space is constituted through the complementary vectors of 'in' and 'out'. When we experience, and talk of, going 'into' ourselves or moving 'out', this dimension may be combined with the others: we go 'down' into ourselves and move out 'towards' other people and the world. Here again, however, conventional language serves an ideological function in distorting and limiting our lived experience of different qualitative movements of awareness. It offers no recognition of the possibility that we can move *inwards* towards others. Or that going into ourselves is, in fact, the very condition of making deeper *inner* contact with others, moving *inwardly* closer to them, and understanding them *from* within. With respect to the in-out polarity, Western culture is clear that centrifugal outward movements are superior to the centripetal movements inward valued in Eastern cultures. Going down into ourselves is valued not as an end in itself but only as a means of restoring our capacity to move out and move on. Western culture identifies outward movement with growth and expansion, inward movement with a contraction of horizons – a spatial prejudice seemingly confirmed by the historic lack of forward 'progress' and 'upwards' economic development in inwardly-oriented or introspective Eastern cultures. With expansion being identified with outward movement, there is no concept of *inward expansion* or 'in-spansion' of awareness – or of how the quality of our outer lives can be enriched through the inward movement of awareness. And yet inward expansion is something we experience each time a dream expands outwards from a point deep within us, and each time our awareness expands by entering more deeply *into* something or someone – or letting them into us more deeply.

Human awareness not only has a variable focus but a variable *locus* or centre. We can not only vary the focus of our awareness but vary its locus. Sensing where our own awareness is spatially centred in our bodies, and sensing the spatial flows and movements of awareness in and around our bodies, tells us where we 'are' in *qualitative space*. Asking another person where they sense *their* awareness to be centred in their bodies, or sensing this in a bodily way ourselves, tells us far more about them than asking them what their intellectual, emotional or moral 'position' is on a particular issue. Sensing the bodily coordinate points of an individual's awareness, and the spatial vectors along which their awareness moves or gets stuck, gives us a much more direct cognition of where a person 'is', where they are 'coming from' and where they are 'going' than anything they may say about themselves.

A coordinate point of awareness in soul-space is nothing abstract. Moving locus of awareness between different coordinate points gives a different quality to the whole 'space' we find ourselves in. Whenever we sense ourselves having made an inner connection with an object, place or person, we establish such a coordinate point in our own awareness. Coordinate points in soul-space are essentially points of resonant *inner contact, connection* and *communication* between things and people. In measurable quantitative space continuum we move *between* one point and another. In qualitative soul-space we establish a resonance between one coordinate point of awareness and another that draws those points together as a single point or 'singularity'. Dream locations are coordinates in qualitative space. So too are physical locations. In the topology of three-dimensional space a coordinate point is defined by linear axes; points are understood as points *on* a line or as intersections of lines. Lines are understood as lines *of* or *between* points. In the topology of qualitative space and the qualia continuum, the zero-dimensional point is both a *first* and a *fourth* dimension. This fifth dimension is the dimension of resonant inner connection between the qualitative soul-spaces inhabited by different beings, and the qualities of awareness that define those spaces.

As singularities, coordinate points of awareness serve as channels through which new qualities of awareness, previously *peripheral* to our consciousness, can become central. Our *tanden* or abdominal centre of awareness is such a singularity – a centre of awareness linking us inwardly with others and with the cosmos as a whole. Our contemporary global culture, however, is one in which human awareness has become dis-located from this centre, in which it has shifted away from the singularity at the core of our being and become centred in a secondary, more peripheral coordinate point of awareness – the centre of awareness we experience in our heads. This is a centre of ego-awareness located in the sensed inner space of our heads, just between the eyes and behind the forehead, and closely associated with *visual* perception of space. Following Eastern spiritual traditions New Age thinking still associates this head centre with a higher 'spiritual' centre or 'third eye'. In fact, its 'spiritual character' derives entirely from the fact that human beings in certain ancient cultures still *lacked* a clear *ego-centred* locus of awareness in the head. It was for this reason that they saw the establishment and strengthening of this centre as their primary spiritual goal – a goal quite inappropriate today, given that this head centre has long since been firmly established as the principal coordinate point of awareness of modern civilisation.

The traditional counter part and counterpoint to the head centre in Western civilisation has always been the heart centre, located in the felt interiority of our chest. Western culture is a contrapunctal fugue of head and heart, intellect and emotion, thought and feeling. Japanese culture, in contrast, was traditionally a culture not of the head or heart but of the belly or *hara* – a centre of awareness located in the felt inner space of the abdomen just below the navel.

As Graf Von Dürckheim explained in his classic book on Japanese hara-culture:

Hara de kangaeru (to think with the belly) is the opposite of *atama de kangaeru* (to think with the head)...The Japanese says, tapping his forehead with his finger 'One must not think with this', and often adds 'Please think with your belly.'

The expression 'thinking with the head' has a similar status to the English expression 'thinking off the top of one's head', implying superficiality and a lacking capacity for patient inward listening and reflection. The fact that supposedly 'scientific' books can now be published with titles such as 'How the brain thinks' shows just how far the *head-thinking* of the West has gone, and how we have lost the understanding that it is *beings* that think and feel, speak and act, breathe and metabolise – not bodies or brains. When we speak of someone thinking with their 'head' or 'heart' or 'hara' it is not activities of the anatomical brain, breast or belly that we are referring to. Such language refers rather to different qualities of awareness reflected in thought – qualities which are sensed as having a different locus, centre or coordinate point in the qualitative inner space of our *felt body*.

While the head is geared to perceive only what it sees outside in the outer world, the inner organism of the human being. The lower organs, are geared to have perceptions in the spiritual world.
Rudolf Steiner

In earlier cultures it was not the brain but the heart, or even lower organs such as the liver that were regarded as the seat of consciousness and the bodily locus of our sense of self. Nowadays we regard such beliefs as almost childish – a sign of anatomical ignorance. We do not consider that they may have been the expression of a felt inner experience of particular organs rather than a claim to anatomical knowledge of them. In modern Western culture, most individuals are so little in touch with their own felt body, and so far removed from a felt bodily sense of self, that they treat their own body as a thing or 'It' rather than as their own embodied self. They are so identified with their mental ego or 'I' that the brain itself is treated as a mere bodily object. As Dürckheim said:

For the prisoner of this 'I', the world has no depth. [In contrast] Self-awareness anchored in hara is awareness of a self larger than the mere 'I'....In hara he participates in a deeper Being which fundamentally is his true nature but from which, in his former condition, in the prison of his 'I', he was cut off.

Speaking of the different qualitative space of awareness that opens up through centring the coordinate point of our awareness in the hara, Dürckheim writes:

> Man's 'way inward' is the way of uniting himself with his Being, wherein he partakes of life beyond space and time....The man without hara has only a very small space within and around him. The man who gains hara enters into a new relationship with the world which makes him both independent of it and yet connected with it in an unforced way...he will unfailingly experience sensations of a new strength, a new breadth and a new nearness and warmth....The man without hara is dependent on the world precisely because he lacks real connection with it; the man with hara is constantly connected to the world because he is independent of it.

Diagram 1 illustrates how the _tanden_ – the coordinate point of awareness in the abdomen or hara – can be represented as both the physical centre of gravity of the human body and is at the same time the spiritual centre of awareness of the human being – one which leads down from the qualitative inner space or felt withinness of our own bodies into a field of unbounded interiority linking us with the withinness of other beings.   _Collective_

Diagram 1

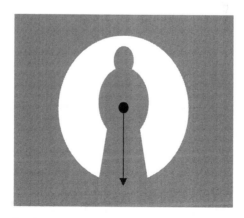

Diagram 2 illustrates the *inner connection* between individuals that can be established through this field, a connection made directly from the hara – the central coordinate point or inner core of our being.

Diagram 2

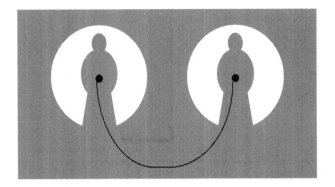

In ordinary life and ordinary dreaming, we experience our movement through qualitative space only subconsciously. We are aware of the different sensual qualities of awareness that we move through only as sensed bodily moods or modes of awareness. We are aware of our inner *motions* in qualitative space only through outward *e-motional* shifts in our sensed bodily moods and modes of awareness. Only in activities in which we need to actively and consciously *attune* ourselves to something or someone – whether engaging in serious conversation, reading a book, playing a musical instrument or practising a sport do we experience a movement of awareness that establishes new coordinate points of awareness – new points of resonance with the things and people around us.

Very few people, however, are capable of consciously *moving* the locus of their awareness and altering its coordinate point. They are not aware of the bodily centre or locus of their own awareness, or aware in a bodily way of the vectors along which they can move it. They may adopt different emotional stances or mental attitudes. They do not realise, however, that intellectual positions and mental points of view are merely the surface *expression* of the coordinate points of an individual's bodily self-awareness, and that emotions are the outward expression of inner motions of awareness between these coordinate points. A person's bodily posture reveals more about their inner world outlook – the 'place' they are coming from in themselves and the 'point' from which they view the world – than any emotional stance or intellectual position. In particular it tells us how head or heart-centred they are, and whether or not they are in contact with the central coordinate point of their own body of awareness – the hara.

In both one-to-one and group relationships, the 'soft spots' that people have for one another, the 'touchy points' or 'sensitive spots' they avoid touching, and the points of deeper 'spiritual' connection that they have with one another are all coordinate points in qualitative space. As individuals our whole lives are nothing more or less than a journey in qualitative space in which we search for *points of resonance* – between self and other, between our inner and outer lives, between our feeling and our thoughts, our impulses and our actions, our felt potentialities and the lived actualities of our existence. This resonance can take the form of 'cognitive resonance', or emotional or 'empathic' resonance, or a deep, inwardly felt 'somatic' or 'organismic' resonance. In essence, we seek resonances between the inner 'space' we find ourselves in, our outer environment, and the qualitative 'spaces' that other people 'in' this same environment are actually 'in'. Particular places and people become important to us because they represent coordinate points of resonance which amplify those qualities of awareness most central to our sense of self. Alternatively they may serve as singularities which open us to new qualities of awareness, expanding our sense of self to embrace new qualities of awareness, healing us through contact with our qualitative entirety or whole self, or restoring a sense of our qualitative essence or quintessential self. What places and people 'mean' to us is what they *are* for us in qualitative space – the qualities of awareness they *express, embody and emanate*. For it is through *resonance* with these soul qualities that we give birth to new coordinate points of awareness in that larger qualitative space or sphere of awareness that we call 'the soul'.

With all deference to the world continuum of space and time, I know as living truth only concrete world reality, which is constantly, in every moment, reached out to me. I can separate it into its component parts, I can compare them and distribute them into groups of similar phenomena, I can derive them from earlier and reduce them to simpler phenomena; and when I have done all this I have not touched my concrete world reality.   Martin Buber

What Buber speaks of as 'concrete world reality' is nothing quantitatively measurable, nor is it composed merely of extensional material bodies 'in' space-time. It consists instead of *qualitative spaces* of the sort we move through each day of our lives, spaces whose coordinates are nothing more nor less than points of resonant inner contact with our concrete outer world.

The topology of qualitative space comes to expression in social life through the dynamics linking individuals in both one-to-one and group relationships. The individual is on the one hand the centre of a unique sphere of awareness, encompassing a unique range of qualities of awareness. As a member of a group, however, the individual is a *peripheral* point on a circle which includes other individuals. At the same time, each individual is a unique *centre* of awareness of the group or organisation as a whole. When an individual becomes a member of a new group or organisation, it opens up for them a larger sphere of awareness. No matter how few people they know, they have a 'peripheral' awareness of the entire group or organisation and all its members. But being themselves a new and unique centre of awareness for the group or organisation as a whole, each member is also uniting and concentrating in a highly individualised way the diverse qualities of awareness embodied by all its other members. Each individual in a group, therefore, like each sub-group within an organisation, speaks not only for themselves but for the group or organisation as a whole, and for each of its other members or sub-groups. No member of a group is ultimately more on its periphery or closer to its centre that any other. Such concepts pertain to organisational structures and their hierarchies but ignore the holarchical dimension of groups – a dimension in which each individual, no matter how 'peripheral' is both a unique centre of awareness for the organisation as a whole and a coordinate point of *inner connection* for a specific sub-group of other members of that organisation. Each individual, moreover, is also a coordinate point of awareness in another way, being a unique point of connection between all the different groups and organisations – ethnic and familial, occupational and professional, social and cultural – to which that individual belongs.

People regarded as *eccentric* have a locus of awareness that is *off-centre* or ex-centric in terms of others. When people feel a sense of inner 'dislocation', this is because the coordinate point of their awareness has indeed been shifted or dislocated. Relocating ourselves in geographical space and/or encountering different cultures or characters with a different coordinate point of awareness can induce such a sense of inner dis-location. The literal meaning of the German word for 'mad' (*verrückt*) is 'dis-located'. According to Heidegger the 'normal' consciousness of modern man is itself a type of madness – a dis-location brought about by an exclusive identification with his head-or heart-centre. Conversely, madness can be seen as a way through which people seek to dis-locate themselves *back* to their true centre in the hara, and in doing so recover the full breadth and depth of their own qualitative space of awareness.

Modern man must first and above all find his way back into the full breadth of the space proper to his essence. That essential space of man's essential being receives the dimension that unites it to something beyond itself...Unless man first establishes himself beforehand in the space proper to his essence and there takes up his dwelling, he will not be capable of anything essential within the destining now holding sway.   Martin Heidegger

The individual's body of awareness is a five-dimensional body configuring a qualitative soul-space. The locus of an individual's awareness within this space is its position in relation to three principal coordinate points of awareness – *head, heart and hara*. These are aligned on a vertical axis along which practitioners of 'energy medicine' identify different 'energy centres' or 'chakras' such as the crown, the throat centre, the solar plexus and a root centre at the base of the spine. The *hara* is often *not* included among these chakras, despite the fact that in both Chinese and Japanese spiritual traditions it was recognised as the physical and spiritual centre of gravity of the human being – not one 'energy centre' among others in an 'energy body' but the deepest and most central coordinate point of awareness in our own overall spatial sphere or *body of awareness*. This body of awareness – the human organism – was understood in the Western Pythagorean tradition as a musical instrument or *organon* comparable to a vertical *monochord* – a single-stringed instrument whose three principal *nodes* are head, heart and hara.

Diagram 3 shows the three nodes of the human monochord in *all* their harmonics, which together give expression to the ground tone or 'fundamental tone' (Seth) of the individual human being.

Diagram 3

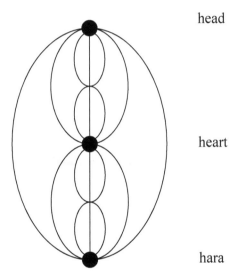

head

heart

hara

It is the positioning of an individual's locus of awareness between the head and hara, and their capacity to freely move the locus of their awareness between these primary nodes, that finds expression in their whole way of being and relating. For each node or coordinate point of awareness represents a qualitatively different mode of awareness of the world and qualitatively different point of contact with it.

Character differences between individuals, groups and organisations, ethnic cultures and historic civilisations all have their basis in different harmonic relationships between the three main nodes of the human monochord, the presence or absence of different subharmonics linking them and the *fixation of* awareness at or between different *dominant* coordinate points of awareness.

Diagrams 4 and 5 show how the characterological structure of an individual or culture can be schematically represented as a monochord in which certain harmonics of the complete monochord are missing, and instead barriers exist between different centres of awareness. The *dominant* centre of awareness characterising an individual and/or culture, and functioning as its coordinate point, is represented by a ringed centre or node of the monochord.

Harmonic links between centres are represented by the curves connecting or not connecting them. Barriers between centres, on the other hand, are represented by bars across the vertical line between them.

Diagram 4 is a schematic representation of the normative individual character structure of a modern Western culture in which the head is the principal centre of awareness, head and heart are harmonically linked, but there is no harmonic linking of head and hara, and there is a barrier between heart and hara.

Diagram 4

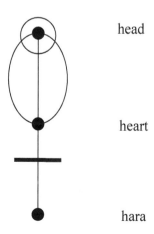

head

heart

hara

In contrast, Diagram 5 represents the normative character structure of *traditional* Japanese culture. Here, the *hara* is the dominant centre, head and *hara* are linked harmonically, as are heart and *hara*, but not so head and heart, which are divided by a barrier.

Diagram 5

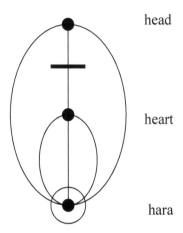

head

heart

hara

The monochord model of the human organism, showing three principal centres or loci of awareness, a dominant centre and harmonics or barriers between centres, can be used to represent a whole variety of typical or ideal character structures. It allows more sophisticated diagrams to be constructed which include additional nodes and harmonics representing other centres of awareness. Such diagrams can also be used to represent the precise *coordinate points* of individual awareness – not identifying these coordinates with dominant centres or nodes but rather indicating their locations *in between* the principal nodes. Their primary deficiency, as two-dimensional schemas, lies in their concentration on the central *vertical* axis of the qualitative space defining our body of awareness. As a result it cannot show loci, coordinate points and flow vectors of an individual's awareness in all four dimensions of qualitative space. To show the true coordinate points of dream consciousness, or of an infant's or child's awareness, diagrams would be necessary which locate the coordinate point of their awareness outside the entire sphere of their inner bodily awareness. The coordinate point of a new born baby's awareness may not yet be located in their outer or inner body space at all but in the 'spiritual world' – the unbounded interiority of the qualia continuum.

For infants and children, other people such as parents and peers, and even inanimate objects such as teddy bears and toys, can function as *external loci* of their own *self-awareness*. Their coordinate point of awareness is still highly mobile, able not only to move along the vertical axis of qualitative space but occupy locations in space outside their bodies. The same mobility that belongs to their coordinate point of awareness also belongs to their entire body of awareness. Their own felt body is one that can easily shift shape, taking on imaginary forms in resonance with their own feeling tones, or becoming isomorphic with the forms of things and people. The child's tendency to spontaneously adopt the vocal, facial and gestural mannerisms of its parents come about through 'morphic resonance' (Sheldrake) – the child's felt inner resonance with the outer form of these mannerisms, and its capacity to give form to this resonance through its own fluid and shape-shifting body of awareness. Paradoxically, it is this very capacity for resonance with its parents that may lead a child to not only *stabilise* its coordinate point of awareness but to fix it, to create barriers between its different centres of awareness and to establish rigid field boundaries between itself and the world around it and quite literally shrink its own outwardly and inwardly expansive body of awareness to the spatial dimensions and shape of its own physical body – or a mere part of that body, its *head,* for example. As a result, it finds no difficulty in then accepting from its teachers a conventional physical scientific world view – one in which both human beings and the cosmos are intellectually reduced to a set of spatially separated bodies which are solidly bounded and more or less like the human head itself.

Our whole notion of perceptual objects as bodies surrounded by empty space comes from identifying their three-dimensional forms as shapings of material substance rather than as shapings of the space surrounding them. Thus we see the human body externally as fleshly substance surrounded by empty space – a 'fact' seemingly confirmed by 'internal' examination which reveals its cellular tissue and organs. In looking at the human body in this way, what we do not see is the human being. Thus, in looking at somebody's head we do not perceive the inner space of awareness in which the thoughts of this being arise. In looking at their chest we do not perceive the inner space of awareness in which they experience feelings. In perceiving their body as a whole we do not perceive the space or spaces of their own inner awareness of their bodies – the space of their subtle inner *proprioception*. Recognising the reality of these inner spaces we might just as well say that our body is not filled space surrounded by empty space but itself a hole or hollow in space.

When asked what they see in Diagram 6 below, most people would say that they see a circle in a white 'space'. When asked 'What colour is the circle?' their answer would be 'grey'. They see the circle as the 'foreground' grey figure set off against a white 'background'. But what defines the circle *as* a circle – as a form or figure – is just as much the white space around it as the grey region within it. From an ordinary spatial point of view the circle is grey. From a 'counter-spatial' perspective it is white. The circle as such, however, is neither grey nor white but is a figure formed by the boundary of the grey and white regions of the diagram. What we actually see, therefore, is just as much a white circle with an empty grey space or hole within it as a grey circle with an empty white space around it.

Diagram 6

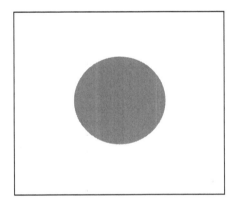

Fanciful though it is, the notion of a 'hollow earth' is an imaginative picture of the true nature of all extensional bodies as the surface boundaries of inner hollows in counter-space surrounding them. It is only externally, however, that these hollows appear as bounded. The qualitative inner soul-space of an extensional body is not bounded but bottomless or unbounded. Inwardly it has no extensional boundaries whatsoever but leads into a realm of unbounded non-extensional interiority.

The 'hollow' soul-space of our own felt body is not an *empty* space, however, but a space 'filled' with awareness – for it is an inner space *of* awareness. Similarly, the space we perceive around us is not empty space but a space filled with awareness, for it is the outer spatial *field* of our sensory awareness. The periphery of our felt body is a boundary between two fields of spatial awareness – the outer field of our spatial awareness of the world and the inner field of our bodily self-awareness. Like the two-dimensional circle drawn in Diagram 7, the three-dimensional sphere that constitutes our body of awareness is defined neither by the inner space of awareness it bounds nor by the spatial field of awareness around it, but it is the peripheral *field-boundary* of those spaces. It is this peripheral field boundary or 'skin' of our own soul-body that first defines an outer and an inner space of awareness. Like the circle, our own body – indeed any body – is identical neither with the matter 'filling' it nor the 'empty' space around it. It is itself a boundary of two *filled spaces* – 'hollow' spaces of awareness 'filled' with *qualities of awareness*.

Diagram 7

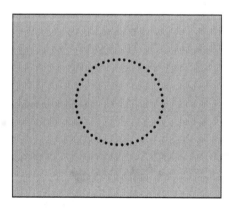

Our psychical or *soul-body* [*internal*] is the felt bodily shape and substantiality of our *self-awareness*. The physical body, on the other hand, is the *externally* perceived form of our body consciousness or *body-soul* – the collective consciousness of the atoms, molecules and cells that make up our bodies. Whereas the perceived boundary of our body-soul remains more or less stable, the peripheral boundary and qualitative inner space of our soul-body can expand, contract and shift shape. Our felt body is influenced by the felt *relation* between our soul-body and body-soul, between the sensed shape and substantiality of our self-awareness on the one hand and, on the other hand, the combined awareness of each of the molecules, cells and organs that make up our physical bodies.

If our self-awareness withdraws inwardly from our physical body boundary, the fleshly shapes and textures *of awareness* that ordinarily make up our body of awareness or soul-body cease to be experienced as such. Instead we become more aware of our own physicality or body-soul. The bodily sensations of fatigue or heaviness before falling asleep represent a heightened consciousness of our physicality and of our body-soul as an independent consciousness in its own right. As our awareness withdraws inwardly from the sensed boundary of our physical bodies, we experience an increased sense of physical heaviness and density, and a dulling of the light of our ordinary waking consciousness. Similarly, if during waking life we withdraw our own awareness from a *part* of our body, we begin to experience it as some 'thing' independent of us. In the extreme case we experience that part of our body as a source of *pain*. For, when a part of our body hurts us, this is because our self-awareness or soul-body no longer fully permeates it to the degree necessary to feel this part of our body as part of our being – our own embodied *self*. What before was felt as a part of our bodily self-awareness – or 'I' – is now felt as some independent body *part* or 'It' that affects us in one way or another. Conversely, the more our self-awareness permeates our body-soul, not in part, but *as a whole*, the more our own bodily sense of self is enhanced, leading to an experience not of pain but of pleasure.

Physical pleasure and pain reflect the felt relation between our soul-body and body-soul. Physical pain is the sensation arising from the localised withdrawal of the soul-body from a *part* of the body-soul – a sensation which in turn recalls awareness to that part. Physical pleasure is essentially a non-localised sensation arising from the intensified permeation by the soul-body of the body-soul as a whole. Thus, the more localised a sensation of pleasure is, the less

96

pleasure we experience. Conversely, the more localised a sensation of pain is, the more we experience it as pain. In going to sleep, our soul-body withdraws from the body-soul, but this is not experienced as pain, for it withdraws from the body-soul as a whole. In the process, however, an involution occurs whereby the relation of soul-body and body-soul is inverted. For, in our dreams the soul-body is itself more or less permeated by qualities and textures of awareness stemming from the body-soul itself. The relation of body-soul and soul-body in our dreams is experienced as a relation of our dreamt body and its dream environment. In the process of awakening, on the other hand, our soul-body begins to once again permeate our body-soul as a whole. What before was experienced as qualities of the outer environment or atmosphere of our dream, lingers on as a residual inner state of our own felt body. In our dreams, qualities belonging to our inwardly felt body take the form of experienced events and environment of the dream, and vice versa. Waking events and environments are 'internalised' and experienced as qualities of our own felt dream body.

In general, what we perceive as physical bodies in space are the outwardly perceived form taken by field-qualities and field-patterns of atomic and molecular awareness. The physical light that reflects off or radiates from these bodies, however, can only be perceived *in the light* of our own awareness of them. The sense organs with which we perceive other bodies in space lie on the perceived periphery of our own physical bodies.

As Steiner recognised, like our ordinary waking awareness of the world, our ordinary understanding of both space and light is *point-centred*, radial and centrifugal. Light is conceived as something that radiates outward from points in space. We have no concept of a *centripetal* movement in a 'counter-space' that radiates inwardly from a periphery. What Steiner called the 'ether body', the peripheral surface of our soul-body or body of awareness, was, he insisted, something 'that is centripetally, rather than centrifugally formed. In your ether body you dwell within the totality of space.'

'In ordinary life, we look outwards from within.' Though we feel enclosed within our physical skins, we are unused to experiencing our bodily periphery as a periphery *of awareness* from which we can *look in* rather than out. Doing so would give us the experience of our own awareness radiating inwardly, and in doing so, opening up and expanding a qualitative inner space of awareness. The soul-body or body of awareness consists of an outer periphery of awareness and inner coordinate points of awareness. Only by identifying with the *peripheral awareness* can we look in from the inner surface of this periphery towards its different centres, or coordinate *points,* in the qualitative inner space that opens up within it. One of these – the hara – is a counter-spatial centre: a 'centre at infinity' or 'inward infinitude' that constitutes the core of our being. But what if not just our own bodies but all bodies are essentially bodies of awareness, with their own qualitative inner and outer spaces of awareness. What if these extensional soul-spaces are inwardly linked to one another through an unbounded *non-extensional* soul-space of awareness – an 'intensional' fifth dimension that constitutes the 'world of soul' as such?

The 'keyhole' schema in diagram 8 shows how an extensional body 'in' an outer space (white) possesses a qualitative inner space or 'hollow' of awareness (grey). Like our hara centre or *tanden*, the central (black) point of this inner soul-space of awareness is an *inward infinitude,* one that leads directly *into* an unbounded intensional soul-space (grey). The keyhole diagram is a key to how the extensional spaces around any body (white) themselves open up *within* such an unbounded, non-extensional soul-space of awareness (grey). The black, bordered periphery of the white area around the circular body represents both the perceived horizon of its outer spatial field and the perceived exteriority of all other bodies within it.

Diagram 8

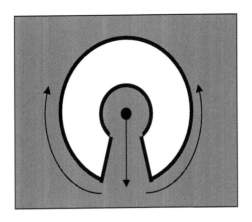

Diagram 9 illustrates how soul science conceives the general relation *between* bodies in space: as a relation between their inner and outer, intensional and extensional fields or soul-spaces of awareness. In this diagram the light grey oval represents a non-extensional source field, plane or domain of awareness (light grey) within the soul world (dark grey). Two circular fields of extensional spatial awareness (white) open up *within* this source field. The source field itself, however, also takes shape within these spaces in the form of the two larger oval figures within them. These figures represent two bodies in space, understood as manifestations of a common non-extensional source field of awareness. As figurations *of* awareness, each body constitutes at the same time an independent consciousness or soul being that configures its own distinct outer fields of spatial awareness – inhabiting its own independent and qualitatively distinct soul-space. The smaller of the grey ovals within each of these spaces is each consciousness's external perception of the other as an extensional body within its own outer field of spatial awareness. The dotted lines represent each of the two consciousness's external perception of each other as bodies 'in' their own respective spatial fields of awareness. The continuous black line, on the other hand, represents their resonant *inner connection* within one another through the non-extensional source field of awareness in which they are both figurations.

Diagram 9

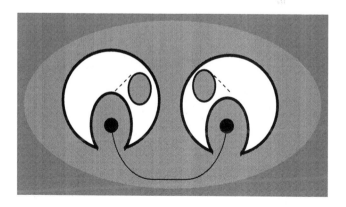

Were we to seek to add a qualitative dimension of colour to this grey schematic picture, each of the two consciousnesses or figurations of awareness would be represented in different colours – representing the fundamental quality or colouration of their awareness. Their colours would diffuse outwardly into the 'white' spaces surrounding them – representing the way in which their respective qualities of awareness give a qualitative colouration to the space around them, and in doing so also colour their external perception of one another. The common source field would cease to be a uniform grey but instead become a gradient of two colours, each of which would reach a maximum intensity in the ovals representing the two soul beings. If all consciousnesses, at all levels, configure and occupy their own distinct and qualitatively unique subjective spaces, how is it that they can perceive themselves as dwelling in a common 'objective' space and a commonly shaped or 'isomorphic' world of bodies in space? Whether and to what extent the perceptual worlds that two or more consciousnesses are aware of are *isomorphic* is determined by the degree of resonance between their respective spatial field patterns and field qualities of awareness – for it is the latter that shape and colour the patterned fields of awareness that constitute their perceptual 'worlds'.

In Diagram 10 the black border of the human figure represents the physical dimension of our bodyhood (black) as a boundary state between an outer soul-space or field of awareness (white) and an inner soul-space of awareness (light grey), both forming part of a singular soul-body or body of awareness whose periphery is the light grey area surrounding the black circle.

Diagram 10

As in diagrams 8 and 9, the black border here represents the externally perceived boundaries of our own bodies, the perceived horizon of the physical space around us – whether the walls of a room or the night sky – and the perceived exteriority of other bodies around us. This light grey area around it however – the periphery of our soul-body – is not a physical boundary but a non-physical *field* boundary or envelope of awareness. It is this outermost field-boundary that constitutes what is often termed the 'astral body'. What is termed the 'ether body' or 'etheric body' on the other hand, is the body-soul or body consciousness as we experience it through our own inwardly felt body (the light grey area within the human figure). As the diagram clearly shows, however, our inwardly felt or etheric body and our 'astral' body are not separate bodies at all, but merely distinct fields of a singular soul-body or body of awareness. As to what is often termed the 'aura', this term merely acknowledges the fact that our soul-body permeates our body-soul and influences the quality energy that it emanates. But the idea that the human aura has measurable *quantitative* extensions or boundaries is a distortion. For, this outer dimension of our felt body never varies in quantitative *extension* but only in the *intensity* of the quality-energy it emanates. Our singular body of awareness, or soul-body, includes not only the inner and outer field of our physical body-soul and felt body, but the larger *peripheral* field of awareness that lies behind all that we perceive in the physical world around us.

Diagram 11 shows how the illusion that as bodies we inhabit a common physical space and a common physical world, can be represented as a merger of the *peripheral* fields or 'astral bodies' of two or more beings. For it is through these peripheral fields that their respective *field-patterns* of awareness enter into *resonance* with one another. And it is through this resonance between the field-patterns of awareness of two or more beings that they create what appears to be a similarly patterned or *isomorphic* perceptual space and perceptual world.

Diagram 11

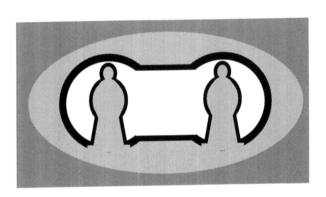

This diagram offers an important clue to the statements of Rudolf Steiner that we are *within* the objects we perceive externally – for we are linked to them not through the qualitative inner soul-space or felt withinness of our own bodies. It also helps explain why we tend to ignore the truth spelled out in another statement of Steiner's – that it is a complete myth to think that our awareness or subjectivity is contained within our skins or bodily boundaries, for it extends outwardly to permeate the space around us and reaches to the very horizons of our perceptual world. It is only because we experience the outer field of our subjective spatial awareness as an *isomorphic* space – a *shared* perceptual world – that we regard it as an 'objective' physical space independent of our own awareness or subjectivity, and see the latter as something bounded and contained by our bodies. As a result, however, we cease to *experience* the way in which our own awareness is both externally and internally *unbounded* by the outwardly perceived physical exteriority of our bodies. The way back to such an experience is through resensitisation to the *field* character of our bodily self-awareness, in particular the three main fields or spheres of awareness that make up the soul-body or body of awareness:

1. the field of *aroundness* which we normally perceive only as shared, objective physical space separating us from others and extending out into the cosmos.
2. the field of *withinness* that we normally experience as a private and subjective inner space, bounded by our own bodies from which we look out at the world.
3. the field of *unbounded interiority* that we normally *do not* experience – because to do so would require that we turn our gaze *inwards* and experience the cosmically unbounded nature of our own inner soul-space.

To get *outside* your universe, you need to travel *inward*, and this represents the only perspective from which valid experimentation... can be carried on. Your so-called scientific, so-called objective experiments can continue for an eternity, but they only probe further and further with camouflage instruments into a camouflage universe. Seth

The vision of space travel to far planets is a metaphor of travel between trans-physical planes and spheres of qualitative space that make up the qualia continuum. This is a challenge that cannot be met by technology using sophisticated futuristic vehicles in which to transport human bodies across vast quantitative distances in extensional or outer space. It can only be met by cultivating the ability of human beings to use the inner soul-space of their own bodily 'vehicles' as a five-dimensional gateway into an unbounded non-extensional soul-space. The countless planes and coordinate points of this unbounded qualitative soul-space are the inner counterparts of all that we perceive as planets and coordinate points in cosmic space. We are used to contrasting science fiction with science fact, unaware that the authors of this fiction may be giving symbolic expression to deeper facts. The 'Stargate' and 'Star Trek' technologies of science fiction, with their 'warp drives' and 'wormholes', have in fact become subjects of current scientific research – for example NASA's actual attempts to conceptualise advanced technologies of space travel through electromagnetic resonance with specific coordinate points in space-time. Such technologies, however, merely symbolise the type of inner resonance which constitutes the basic medium of travel through the qualitative soul-space – a resonance between coordinate points of awareness within and beyond our own soul-body. The soul-space of the lower belly or hara and its central coordinate point, the tanden, are points of resonance or inner connection, not only with our own inner selves and those of others, but with the inner cosmos – the aware inwardness of the cosmos as such and of all that we perceive as cosmic bodies in space. We are not simply aware of a cosmos 'out there'. Our awareness extends to the very horizons of that cosmos. We are linked to it directly through a cosmos of awareness 'in here', centred in our hara. The cosmos we are aware of 'out there' is itself an aware cosmos – for every body within it possesses its own aware interiority and its own coordinate point in the unbounded soul-space of the inner cosmos.

Ordinary three-dimensional space has itself a hidden fourth dimension – the fourth being the relation of point and periphery, inwardness and outwardness. As Rudolf Steiner pointed out, what we call the 'fourth dimension' is best understood as a negative of the ordinary relation of point and periphery, inwardness and outwardness, in our experience of three-dimensional space. We are 'in' the fourth dimension whenever we experience ourselves *looking in* from a peripheral field-boundary of awareness rather than looking out at the world from a point or centre of awareness. The 'light of awareness' is its outward radiation from a central point towards an infinite periphery. What we call 'darkness' on the other hand, is no mere lack of light. It is the *inward radiation* of awareness from a periphery towards a point at infinity – an 'inward infinitude'. The *tanden* is such an inward infinitude – a point at infinity towards which an invisible 'dark light' radiates inwards from the cosmos. As such it is also a type of inter-dimensional portal between different three-dimensional realities, linking them not outwardly but inwardly. If the fourth dimension is a negative 'counter-spatial' dimension of ordinary Euclidean space in which the relation of point and periphery is reversed, then its dimensionless 'points at infinity' can be compared to wormholes – four-dimensional conduits which link different three-dimensional realities in a fifth dimension. The fifth dimension is the unbounded non-extensional dimension of spatial *awareness* which we access through the hara. The *hara* is what links the infinite depths of our own *inwardness* with the inwardness of the people around us, and allows us to directly experience the nature of *their* awareness of the three-dimensional world around them from within. As our central coordinate point of awareness it is an inter-dimensional portal – a point of resonant *inner connection* with all that we perceive around us in physical and cosmic space.

Every coordinate point in soul-space is the centre of a three-dimensional *sphere* of awareness. In ordinary three-dimensional space, points are connected by lines or curves, or constitute points of the intersection of those lines and curves. In soul-space, every point is not only the centre of its own sphere of awareness, but the very point of connection between multiple spheres. It is not one-dimensional lines that connect the central points of different spheres of awareness. Instead it is the zero-dimensional points themselves that constitute the link between these spheres in the fifth dimension. For, through its *resonant* inner connection with other coordinate points in this dimension, any given coordinate point can become a *concentric* or *common* centre for multiple spheres of awareness. The space of our felt inner resonance with another person, or a piece of music, belongs to a sphere of awareness quite distinct from the physical space in which sound waves travel as vibrations of air molecules. Resonance is not a mechanical oscillation or vibration. In our dreams we enter into resonance with many different aspects of ourselves, many different coordinate points of our own awareness. As a result we inhabit, and pass through, many different spatial spheres of awareness without leaving our beds.

Primordial images of the cosmos always pictured it as a series of concentric circles or spheres surrounding the earth, with cosmic bodies such as planets being understood as signs or symbols of different spheres of awareness. We all know the difference between the inwardness of a book – the unique sphere of awareness we enter into by reading it – and its outward, three-dimensional form. We all know that having put the book down, we can retain an inner sense of resonant connectedness with this sphere. Even as an object, a purely physical phenomenon, the book would not be a book were it not the three-dimensional surface of an invisible inner sphere of awareness. A book is the outwardly bounded physical manifestation of that inwardly unbounded sphere of awareness inhabited by its author and shared with its readers. A *primordial phenomenon* is a phenomenon in the primordial sense. It is that which comes to light or 'shines forth' (*phainesthai*) through a physical phenomenon – in the same way that an entire sphere of awareness manifests physically and comes to light through the printed or spoken word. Were we to understand all bodies, human and natural, microcosmic and macrocosmic, as primordial phenomenon in this sense, our understanding of the cosmos would alter dramatically – not through new understandings of the outer relationships between such bodies but through establishing a new inner relationship to them.

> Eyes and ears are poor witness for men
> if they do not understand their language.

Heraclitus

Were we to stare at a book as at any other physical object in space, 'studying' its physical dimensions and properties, we would never learn to understand the book in the same way we do when reading it. Were we to research the oscillations of air molecules produced by the sound waves of speech we would remain deaf to what was being said to us – the *Dao* of the word. To truly hear what is said requires us to listen with more than just our heads and hearts, for it is only through the *hara* that we can establish a resonant inner connection with the being addressing us, and in doing so enter the sphere of awareness from which their words first emerge (*phusis*) as physical sounds in space. To hear from the hara means not only looking but *listening in* to a still point of silence within us. This still point of silence is not only the central point of our own cosmic *soul sphere* of awareness. It is a 'third' ear linking us to the music of the spheres.

SPIRIT, SOUL AND *SOMA*

The Unifying Wisdom

of

East and West

Why does 'spirit' matter?

The material world, so we are told, is nothing but a world of energy. The word 'energy' however, is rooted to the Greek word for 'activity' (*energein*) and related to the Greek word for 'work' (*ergon*). It referred to the active and creative *working* of beings. The world, like the word, is a result of the spiritual *working* of beings. So, why does 'spirit' matter? Spirit matters because it is literally that which *matters* – *materialising* as movements of bodies in space and time. It does so in the same way that something we mean to say or do manifests as patterns of bodily movement or vibration in physical space. Spirit is not only what matters, but what *bodies*. It is *not* something we *ascend* to by leaving our bodies, raising our vibrations above those of 'coarse' matter, or entering a mental sphere of lofty thoughts and abstractions. On the contrary, it is that which we *embody* in our own unique way of being and relating to others in the world. The relation of *body, soul and spirit* is analogous to the relation between a book as a visible material body, the invisible space of *meaning* that opens up within that book, and the invisible being that is its author. The world of spirit and soul is a world of beings and of meaning. Our scientific incapacity to acknowledge this world is, as Rudolf Steiner pointed out, a type of soul-spiritual *illiteracy*. To attempt to prove this 'mystical' truth to the modern scientist is, as I constantly emphasise, like attempting to prove to those for whom *reading* is a total mystery that behind the visible pages of a book lies an invisible world of meaning. For meaning *as such* is nothing visible, and neither is the human *being* as such.

Why 'Spirit Soul and Soma'?

Just as physical-scientific research could never find evidence of *meaning* in a text by chemical analysis of its ink and paper, so it can never find evidence of the human *being* by external or internal examination of the human body. Similarly, no physical analysis of the sound vibrations produced by musical instruments, or the human vocal instrument, can reveal their meaning for the human being. We dwell within the world in the same way that we dwell within the word: finding it hollow and empty or full and resonant with meaning. The space of our felt resonance with the spoken word, or a piece of music, is not a physical space but a resonant inner soul-space of directly sensed meaning. And yet the human body, like a book, is not *just* a material body but also a *body of meaning* – composed of fleshly tissues and textures of meaning with their own sensual shape and spiritual substantiality. How else could meaning be felt as *food* for the soul. As we know, however, huge numbers of people today suffer from a type of meaning loss or starvation which they experience as anxiety or depression, or express through a whole variety of 'disorders' or 'diseases'. Medicine and psychiatry classify these as either 'mental', 'physical' or 'psychosomatic'. But the essential nature of human *dis-ease* has nothing to do with 'mind and body', 'psyche' and 'soma' as these words are ordinarily understood. Paradoxically, what is thought of as 'psychosomatic' illness is, in essence, the expression of a complete loss of contact with the *somatic* and *psychical* dimensions of both 'mind' and 'body'. It is a type of soul-spiritual amnesia in which we no longer experience our own inwardly sensed body – the *soma* – as a psychical space of inwardly sensed meaning – the essential *soul-space* in which we dwell as beings. Nor, then, do we experience our own inwardly sensed body as a distinct inner body in its own right – a body of soul and spirit. This amnesia goes so far that we live in the world like immigrants who can never be fully at home in their new country, not because they are nostalgic for their spiritual homeland but because they have completely *forgotten* it – or believe that it is only a myth. Our common spiritual home is the soul world we inhabited before birth, the world we will inhabit again after death, and the world we never cease to inhabit in the depths of our soul – depths that we are normally asleep to, or glimpse only in our dreams. If we cannot accept the heritage we bring with us from our homeworld of soul and spirit, how can we feel fully at home in this one? Dreaming and meditation both offer a tangible, somatic experience of our own soul and spirit. To feel at home and at ease in our own bodies, we need to retrieve the inner *somatic* sense of our own soul and spirit.

What is spiritual knowledge?

What passes today as 'scientific' knowledge tells us that the existence of a world of soul and spirit cannot be proven, and that we must therefore get along with understanding ourselves in a materialist way – not as beings, but just as functional, genetically programmed bodies and minds. Spiritual knowledge, on the other hand, is gnosis – a Greek word which meant knowledge by familiarity or acquaintance. In its spiritual connotation, it refers to the type of direct *relational* knowing we refer to when we speak of knowing someone well or intimately – not merely knowing something *about* them. Gnosis is first-hand not second-hand knowledge; knowledge of someone – a being – and not merely some 'thing'. The subversive 'gnostic' spiritual tradition which we know of through the Mandaean scriptures and the Gnostic Gospels found at Nag Hammadi were concerned with knowing the essential nature of the human being. Here, they recognised a fundamental duality between the outer and the *inner* human being. They recognised the inner human being not simply as an inner 'part' of the outer human being but as a soul-spiritual being in its own right. Gnostic spirituality understands the outer human being as one expression of an inner spiritual self, quite distinct from our outer 'I' or ego. It knows this being as a link between our ordinary *being in the world*, on the one hand, and an entire spiritual *world of beings* on the other.

The more we come to *know* the essential difference between the inner and outer aspects of the human being, however, the more we understand how it is that the human body and mind can come to be experienced as a prison of soul and spirit – how our *being in the world* can be felt as a type of homelessness or spiritual exile. By 'world' the early gnostics did not mean the natural world but the world as fashioned by the human ego. They saw the outer ego of the human being worshipped as a 'god' that called on man not only to rule nature but to rule his own inner nature – to rule his own body and soul, rule the social body and suppress any awareness of an *individual* soul-spiritual self and soul-spiritual body. Yet it is precisely this soul-spiritual body that can re-link the outer human being and human body with the inner human being. The result will be the creation of a newly spiritualised ego and a newly spiritualised sense of our own bodyhood, one ensouled with knowledge of our inner being in all its aspects. Christian spiritual knowledge, or *gnosis*, recognised it as the 'resurrection body' or *soma-pneumatikos*, Buddhist wisdom as the Dharma body, and Daoist alchemy as an embryonic inner body – the 'golden embryo'.

Like the ancient 'world' of the gnostics, the modern 'world' of global capitalist society is identical neither with the earth and natural world, nor the world of soul and spirit. 'World' today means only the worldwide, global market. The earth and its beings have been reduced to a stock of raw materials and exploitable 'resources' – human and animal, vegetable and mineral. The sea is seen as no more than a vast fish farm; animals are herded into concentration camps for processing into food; trees are merely raw materials for the timber industry. Human beings themselves are disposed of as a stock of human 'resources', of exploitable skills and labour power. The work of human beings in capitalist society consists in creating purely quantitative *economic* values, rather than materialising their innermost spiritual values – giving expression to their individual *qualities* of soul. The values of global capitalism are purely *symbolic* values – money and commodities, brands, and the corporate logo. It is brands not beings that are honestly regarded as having 'souls'. Everything of deep spiritual value in the soul life of human beings, and all deep human soul qualities, are perverted by advertising into hollow, flat-screen images of themselves – identified with commodities which merely *symbolise* those soul qualities. The individual soul qualities that individuals embody in their labour, as producers, are exploited and sold back to them as consumers, in the form of commodities.

What is spiritual ignorance?

The early gnostics saw the human body, mind and soul as something that had become distorted through the rule of an all-dominating ego and its god, a god that says "I am I", but knows no *other*. At the heart of gnostic spirituality is the understanding that the inner human being is a spiritual being, one *other* than the ego and the personal, human self we know. The outer human being, in all its aspects, is one human embodiment or incarnation of the inner human being. What we call 'evil' is the result of man's spiritual estrangement or alienation from his inner being, which he comes to regard as an alien being or an evil demonic force. The word 'demon' comes from the Greek *daemon*, which referred to a being neither human nor divine but a guiding spirit or inner voice. Today, we hear of murderers being impelled by inner voices; however, these are not the voice of the *daemon* but of an alter ego that has taken the place of an individual's sense of their own inner being. Out of touch with their inner being – or finding no acknowledgement for it in our secular, materialistic world – individuals are driven to violence in a desperate attempt to penetrate the flesh of others and cut through to their spiritual core. Such violence is both unforgivable and inevitable in a culture which denies any recognition of man's inner being and is ignorant of its spiritual nature. Gnosticism understands 'evil' not as an inherent *part* of man's soul-spiritual nature but as an expression of spiritual ignorance. Spiritual ignorance – *a-gnosis* and *a-gnosticism* – is the denial of man's inner soul-spiritual nature and soul-spiritual body. It is also an ignorance of the *trans-physical*, *trans-personal* and *trans-human* nature of man's inner soul-spiritual being. This ignorance takes many forms:

1. The ignorance that denies the *trans-personal* nature of our inner being and identifies it instead with a divine or semi-divine *person* – a *personified* god, prophet or saviour. This is the ignorance of *traditional religion.*

2. The ignorance that confuses the *trans-personal* dimension of our inner being with an *impersonal energy* or universal life force. This is the ignorance of New Age energy medicine and the ideology of *energeticism.*

3. The ignorance that reduces the inner human *being* to the human *body* and *brain*. This is the ignorance of materialistic science and biological medicine, now expressed in the ideology of *geneticism.*

4. The ignorance that equates the *trans-human* dimension of our inner being with an *inhuman being* – an evil or demonic force, or an extra-terrestrial or *alien being*. This is the ignorance of Satanism, UFO-ism and Alien-style science fiction.

5. The ignorance that opposes the trans-personal and trans-human self to our personal, human self – attempting to affirm the former by violating or sacrificing the latter. This is the ignorance of spiritual martyrdom.

6. The ignorance that identifies the inner human being with a set of cognitive patterns or an internalised parent figure, a set of unconscious instinctual drives or the mythological archetypes of a 'collective' unconscious. This is the ignorance of *psychologism* and *psychoanalysis.*

7. The ignorance that identifies the inner human being with the outer ego (the ignorance of the 'normal' person) or with the inner voice of some super-ego or alter ego (the ignorance of the 'schizophrenic'). Normality and schizophrenia are thus two expressions of the same spiritual ignorance.

8. The ignorance that does not recognise the individual nature of our inner being or inner self, but identifies it instead with the symbols and collective 'spirit' of a particular ethnic group, religious cult or national culture. This is the dangerous spiritual ignorance of *racism* and *nationalism.*

What *maintains* these eight forms of soul-spiritual ignorance is a ninth – an ignorance of the inner human body or *soma*. For it is this soul-spiritual body that can once more re-link the outer and the inner human being. What I call 'soma-spirituality' and 'soma-psychology' is the awakening of an entirely new *bodily* sense of self, one ensouled with knowledge of our innermost spiritual being.

What is the task of spiritual thinking?

Spiritual concepts are a result of spiritual thinking. But spiritual thinking is not simply thinking about 'spiritual' matters, or thinking about things in a 'spiritual' way. Indeed it is not thinking 'about' any 'thing' at all. When we think *about* something our awareness is focussed on what it is we are thinking about – on the 'objects' of our thoughts. Because of this, we cease to be aware of our thought process itself – and in this sense cease to actually think. Spiritual thinking is not *thing focussed* but *thought aware*. It is not a thought governed awareness but an aware thinking. It is awareness of our thoughts that allows us to sense something as-yet *unthought* in the 'things' we think about. Without awareness we can think *about* such things as 'mind' and 'body', 'soul' and 'spirit', 'energy' and 'matter' without ever questioning what these words essentially mean – without every asking what 'mind' and 'body', 'soul' and 'spirit', 'energy' and 'matter' essentially *are*. Instead we take them for granted as 'things'. Spiritual thinking, as aware thinking, cannot rest content with taking things such as 'soul' and 'spirit' for granted and merely thinking about them. Instead it must question the way these 'things' are conventionally thought of, and do so with awareness – from a felt inner sense of their essential meaning (or soul) and their essential being (or spirit). This *inner sense* of what words essentially *mean* and what the things they refer to essentially *are* is a tangible bodily or somatic sense. It comes from our body's own inner knowing or *gnosis* and from knowing our own soul-spiritual body or *soma*. Spiritual thinking is a thinking that is 'spiritual' only because it arises directly *from and within* the soul depths of our own spiritual body. It is not disembodied or soul-less, intellectual or scientific thinking but a soulful thinking that is somatically toned and textured. That is also why it is the only type of thinking that can understand what 'soul, spirit and soma' are.

What are 'Soul' and 'Spirit'?

Just as there are flows of air between and around bodies in space, so are there flows of awareness. Just as we breathe air into and out of the inner spaces of our bodies, so do we breathe in and breathe out awareness. Just as the air we breathe in circulates through our bodies so does awareness. There is, therefore, a good and deep reason why the root meaning of the Greek word *psyche* was 'life-breath', and why the words 'spirit' and 'respiration' have a common derivation from the Latin *spirare* – to breathe. *Psyche*, the Greek word for soul meant 'life breath'. *Pneuma,* the Greek word for spirit, meant also wind – the air around us. At what point does the air around us, the air we breathe in or 'inspire', become part of us – of who we are? At what point does the air we expire cease to be a part of us, becoming simply 'air'? Spiritual traditions of both East and West have long connected our spirit with respiration, and our *awareness of breathing* with something akin to a *breathing of awareness*. Long before 'body' and 'soul', 'mind' and 'spirit' were conceived as separate 'things', there was a felt understanding of the intimate inner relation between the flow and circulation of *air* in and around our bodies, and the flow and circulation of *awareness*. Flows of awareness were felt to posses their own *spiritual substantiality*, constituting a medium which, like air, linked the inwardly sensed inner spaces of our bodies into which we draw breath, with the sensory world around us, in which this air circulates as wind or *pneuma*. There was, therefore, a felt sense of 'spirit' as a medium of meaningful interconnectedness between the aware inwardness of all beings – their soul or *psyche*. This understanding was and is confirmed by the fact that all living beings *breathe,* and that human beings, in particular, express themselves through those shaped and toned flows of breath that constitute *speech*. It was in this sense that the human body itself could be understood as a body *of* soul and spirit – its fleshly 'word' or 'speech'. It was in this sense too, that *spirit* was understood as that which, like the breath we draw in, quite literally *ensouls* the body – allowing the human being to breathe in and vitalise their *awareness* of themselves and the world.

What are 'Body, Mind and Spirit'?

Today the words 'body', 'mind' and 'spirit' have become *soul-less* terms emptied of meaning. For all the talk of 'holistic' approaches to medicine, they are still thought of as referring to three separable 'parts' of the 'whole' human being. Mind and body are understood without reference to soul and spirit. More importantly, no distinction is made between:

1. our physical body and our physical soul or 'body-soul'
2. our body-soul or *soma-psyche* and our mind-soul or *mind-psyche*
3. our body- and mind-souls, and our resonant and spiritual souls
4. our body-soul or *soma-psyche* and our soul-body or *psyche-soma*
   – the inwardly sensed shape and tone of our *resonant soul*
5. our mind-spirit, mental 'I' or *ego* with its centre in our heads and
   our *body-spirit* with its abode in the abdomen or *hara*

All these multiple aspects of the human being are, in the last analysis, determined by a *singular relation* – a relation of inwardness and outwardness, centre and periphery. The soul is the sensed and resonant inwardness of both mind and body – just as meaning is the sensed and resonant inwardness of the word. The unbounded dimension of this inwardness is spirit or *pneuma*. Mind and body are nothing but peripheral boundaries of soul and spirit.

What we perceive as the human body is simply the outwardly perceived and peripheral form of the body's own soul or *body-soul*, this being the collective or gestalt awareness of each of its molecules, cells and organs. The awareness of each atom and cell of our bodies, however, exists not just as a material but as a spiritual unit, possessing its own individualised spirit or quintessence, and its own spiritual substantiality. The body-soul (*soma-psyche* or *soma-psychikos*) is an expression of the spiritual body or *soma-pneumatikos*. The flesh or *sarx* is its outer sensory skin or outwardness. But our body-soul also has an inner surface. This inner surface serves as the *womb* of our own resonant soul, for it is the very boundary between our inwardly sensed body and our inner bodily self-awareness. Music can affect our flesh and permeate our body-soul as vibration without affecting us – without echoing as tones of feeling in our resonant soul.

What we think of as the human 'mind' is a peripheral 'ego skin' (Anzieu) – a skin of language that serves to mirror the felt tones and textures of awareness that make up our resonant soul. The resonant soul is the psychical interiority, not just of our minds and heads, but of our bodies as whole – though it is not normally experienced as such. This is due to the so-called 'mind-body' split – in essence a split between the inner 'mind space' of our heads (the *mind-soul*) and the resonant inner soul-space of our sensed body as a whole, including our chests, belly and abdomen. The resonant soul has its spiritual centre in the *hara* – connecting us to our innermost being and other beings, and providing a portal to the spiritual soul.

What is Soma-Spirituality?

Soma-spirituality is the key to a new spiritual physiology and psychology of the human body. By this I mean not just a new theory but a newly awakening sense of our own body as a spiritual body (*soma-pneumatikos*) one whose inwardness of soul (*soma-psychikos*) links us with the inwardness of every thing and every body around us. Soma-spirituality is the *unifying wisdom of East and West*. It links the Christian understanding of a newly spiritualised body or *soma-pneumatikos* with the Buddhist understanding of the Dharma body, and the 'embryonic body' of Daoist internal alchemy.

> *...perhaps the entire evolution of the spirit is a question of the body; it is the history of the emergence of a higher body that emerges into our sensibility.*

These words of Nietzsche, that self-proclaimed philosophical 'anti-Christ', mirror the mystical essence of Christian spirituality – the resurrection of the flesh (*sarx*) as a newly spiritualised body (*soma*). What is required for this resurrection is a breakdown of the inner barrier between 'head' and 'hara', our mind-spirit and our body-spirit, our mind soul and the resonant interiority of our body-soul. The result is a unification of mind and body through the *resonant soul*, a renewed sense of its connection to our *spiritual soul*, and a renewed experience too, of the *spiritual substantiality* of our own flesh. It is this 'transubstantiation' of the flesh that allows us to experience it not as a physical skin but as a spiritual membrane – one through which we can breathe in the light of our *sensory awareness* of the world around us, absorb the spiritual currents that surround us as air (*pneuma*), and take them into our souls as light- and life-giving breath (*psyche*).

What is the body of soul and spirit?

In the Greek language of the New Testament we find an important distinction between the body as *sarx* ('flesh') and the body as *soma*. *Sarx* meant a sensory surface or *skin* of a body. This was closely related to the outward form or aspect under which any body appeared, understood in Greek thinking as its *eidos* (aspect) or 'idea'. But as the New Testament states "Life is more than meat and the soma more than its raiment" Luke 12.23. The Greek word *soma* referred both to the soul of a body (*soma psychikos*) and to its spiritual substantiality (*soma pneumatikos*). For, long before atomism was associated with 'materialism', matter itself was understood as being composed of the same basic spiritual units as air or *pneuma* – indivisible units, each with their own unique combination of elemental qualities. 'Spirit' as such, therefore, was nothing more nor less than the *individualising* element – that qualitative essence or quintessence of things that endowed them with beingness. 'Soul' was their inwardness – an inwardness not to be understood in an ordinary spatial sense but as something akin to the inwardness of the *word* – its felt inner sense or 'resonance', *meaning*

The Greek word for 'flesh' (sarx) has the literal meaning of 'skin'. Spiritual anatomy understands the human body as a body of soul and spirit. The anatomy of this body can be pictured as a series of concentric skins, each of which constitutes a distinct body (*soma*) in its own right – a surface periphery surrounding and surrounded by a distinct soul-space or sphere of awareness. The most inward of these concentric skins or spheres of awareness is the hara – the abode of our resonant soul and its spiritual core.

Diagram 1

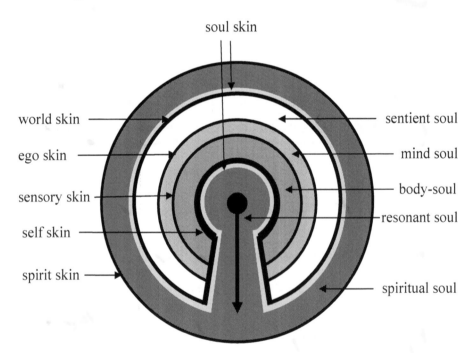

What is here represented as the outermost 'spirit skin' of our soul-spiritual body is simply a field boundary between one of *numberless spheres of awareness*. Known in the past as *aeons*, these spheres constitute both a larger dimension of our own spiritual soul, and concentric spiritual spheres or regions of the soul world as such. Note that the resonant soul, the innermost sphere of our soul-body, is connected through its own centre to our spiritual soul, and that this spiritual soul is what lies behind the 'world skin' of our sensory environment. What the diagram seeks to represent is the way in which, looking into our resonant souls from the inner surface of our self skin, our awareness can flow into the soul-space of awareness that lies *beyond and behind* the outermost horizons of cosmic space that we are aware of through our sensory skin and sentient soul. Note also, that in this diagram the *inner surface* of the self skin surrounding the resonant soul is a *soul skin* contiguous with the *world skin* – the sensory surface of the physical world we perceive around us in space. What this aspect of the diagram represents is the way the soul skin that surrounds the incarnate portion of our spiritual soul is contiguous with the outer surface of our larger soul-body – the astral body. What we sense with this outer soul skin are the very spiritual qualities of soul that manifest as the world skin of our sensory environment. The contiguity of the soul skin and world skin allows our own subtle proprioception of our inwardly sensed body, and self, to link us with all that lies behind the sensory world around us. Our soul-body, as such, is constituted by a singular *soul skin* from which we both look into our own resonant souls, and become sensitive to the world of soul and spirit.

In waking life, our awareness dwells primarily in the spatial spheres of awareness that constitute our sentient soul and mind-soul. The ego skin serves as an 'excitation screen' filtering sensory impressions. It also acts as a mental surface reflecting our sensory awareness of the world in the inner space of the *mind-psyche*. Beneath the skin of our sensory awareness lie the different layers of somatic sensation that derive from our body-soul or *soma-psychatikos*. But this body-soul too, has its own psychic interiority – our resonant soul, filled with the fluid medium of our feeling tone. Just as a singer can be more or less aware of the spacious and sonorous cavities of their physical body, so they – and we – can be more or less aware of our own resonant soul. This awareness can only come from the *inner surface* of our self skin, that part of our inwardly sensed body that makes up the boundary between our body-soul and our resonant soul. The part of us that looks inward from the inner surface of the self skin is our own *inwardly* sensed self or sensed 'inner self'.

We may screen out sensory impression with our ego skin or self skin or allow them to get 'under' our sensory skin. When they do so, we may react from the *outer surface* of our self skin, experiencing the 'autonomic' sensations and 'automatic' thoughts that arise from our body-soul and are reflected by our ego skin. What we normally experience as 'emotions' are motions of awareness rising from the *outer* surface of our self-skin and moving outwards toward our sensory skin and ego skin. It is only when we allow what we experience to get under our self-skin that we can replace reactive responses that come from our self skin with authentic *autonomous* responses that come from our resonant soul and arise from our felt inner *resonance* with things and people.

Feeling tones emanating from our resonant soul permeate our body-soul, influencing cell, muscle and organ tone. They reach outward to the *sensory* surface of our body-soul, which is also the *expressive* surface or face of our resonant soul – manifest in our face and eyes. The sensory skin is not just a sensory or expressive surface, but, like our own skin, a respiratory surface. Through our sensory skin we both breathe in our awareness of the world around us, and emanate qualities of our inner self-awareness.

What is spiritual breathing?

'Respiration' is not merely a biological function but the embodiment of a primordial capacity of our being – the capacity to engage in a rhythmic exchange with the essential 'atmosphere' of our life-world, 'breathing in' our *awareness* of it, drawing inspiration and meaning from it, and in turn allowing our *awareness* to flow out into it and find meaning within it. A person can jog or exercise, or practice Yogic breathing exercises for hours, days or years without it significantly affecting their essential respiration – without it bringing new sources of spiritual meaning and inspiration into their lives. But a person can be neither *inspired* nor *dispirited* without it being instantaneously embodied in their *respiration*. When we breathe into our awareness a 'breathtaking' landscape, idea or emotion, we feel moved to inhale and exhale deeply. Why? Because physical breathing is the embodiment of our primordial capacity to fully absorb and take into *ourselves* our awareness of something or someone other than self, and let this awareness resonate in our souls. The words *respiration, inspiration, expiration, aspiration* etc. all come from the Latin *spirare* – to breathe, just as the Greek word *psyche* originally meant the 'life breath' that vitalised an otherwise lifeless corpse, and left it at death. To speak in a modern scientific way of the 'psychosomatic' dimension of somatic breathing disorders such as asthma, or their 'psychogenic' causation, therefore misses the point entirely – ignoring the central question of what breathing itself essentially *is*. In its most essential sense respiration is not a physiological 'function' of our body at all, but rather a basic psychical capacity of our *being*. This is a capacity exercised through our *respiratory body* – our *spiritual body*. Dispiritedness and inspiration are not disembodied 'psychological' states of mind that then 'affect' our bodily breathing – they are themselves *soma-spiritual* and *soma-psychological* states, states of our spiritual and psychical *body*. Many Eastern traditions use awareness of breathing and meditational breathing techniques to cultivate spiritual awareness. Such breathing techniques are useless, however, without an understanding of their true purpose, which is to spiritualise our breathing itself, and experience it as spiritual activity of our own body of soul and spirit. To spiritualise our breathing means not only being more aware of our breathing. It means to transform our awareness of breathing into a *breathing of awareness*. This is the essential purpose of hara breathing (see *Introduction to Hara Awareness*).

What is spiritual soul resonance?

'Spirit' is the quintessential *individualising* dimension of both inner soul qualities and outer sensory qualities. Its element is *tone*; the unique tonality of this person's voice or this object's colour, for example. 'Mind' is the *formative* dimension of both soul qualities and sensory qualities. Mind is the essence of energy as the formative, patterning activity (*energein*) through which spirit *matters*. 'Soul' itself is the dimension in which pattern and tone combine to resonate as patterned tones – as meaningful sound and speech, song and music. The world of soul is a world of resonant meaning. Soul is 'inter-being' or 'field being' – our capacity for meaningful resonance with our own being and other beings in their spiritual individuality. Even a material object such as a book possesses, like the human body, its own spiritual individuality or beingness. It is not just a structure of atoms and molecules. It is a highly *individualised* field-pattern of atomic and molecular *awareness*. In its own way the book, no less than a bird, knows itself as a being. The world of spirit is a world of individual beings. What we call 'spirituality' is our capacity to resonate with the qualitative spiritual essence or quintessence of things and people – their beingness. Just as it makes a difference whether we see an object as 'red' or attend and attune to the unique *tone* of the object's redness, so it makes all the difference whether we perceive an object as a 'book' or attune to the unique overall tonality of all its sensual qualities. By doing so, we bring ourselves into inner resonance with its essential individuality or *beingness*. At the core of the spiritual teachings in this book is a fundamental distinction between the human body, on the one hand, and the inner human being on the other. Just as speech is an outer expression of the human being, so is the human body its fleshly text. The meaning that ensouls the spoken or written word, like that which ensouls a song or piece of music does not ever die, but endures – continuing to resonate in the soul of the listener.

What is spiritual communication?

In the soul-spiritual world from whence we come, to which we return at death – and which, in an important sense, we never leave – communication with other beings takes the form of wordless soul resonance. Its medium is not audible sound tones but soundless tones of feeling – soul tones. We ride and 'read' our felt resonance with other beings, as we might ride our resonance with a piece of music and 'read' the wordless meanings it conveys. In this world, music is a universal language. In that world, feeling tones are the medium of musical resonance linking one soul with another. They do not simply travel through us like surface emotions that rise and fall, come and go. Instead we travel through them, transported as by music into those qualitative dimensions of our own soul that constitute our resonant link with other souls and the world of soul. The visual landscapes of the soul world, like the visual images that may arise when we listen to music, dream or read a book are all expressions of soul resonance – the inner music of the soul. Behind the *visual world* of our dreams themselves is a *tonal world*. And if dreams are a type of stage on which we allow ourselves to personify and dramatise our life of soul, then beneath this stage is an inner orchestra. The music it plays – the music of feeling tone – is what then finds expression in the nightly dramas of our dreams.

Each person's qualities of soul, their warmth or coolness, brightness or darkness, heaviness or lightness of soul are the expression of inner soul tones with those qualities. Soul-spiritual communication does not consist of meanings represented *in* words, but of resonant tonal qualities of soul communicated *through* the word (*dia-logos*) and conveyed by its *silent undertones*. This is a type of communication that can only be understood in the same way we understand music – through inner resonance. But ours is a visual and verbal culture in which communication, even in the special settings of counselling and psychotherapy, lacks the musical dimension of soul and spirit. That is why people need the healing power of music more than medicine or counselling – for through music they can re-enter the womb of their own resonant soul and listen to *its* language.

Soma-psychology allows us to distinguish three distinct levels of human communication. Diagram 2 is a simplified model of the *body* of soul and spirit, divided into three distinct spheres: a 'mind sphere' with a verbal thought skin as its surface, a 'body' sphere bounded by our sensory and emotional skin, and an inner soul sphere of our overall soul and spirit. These three spheres also correspond to the three main centres of awareness in this body - *head, heart and hara*.

Diagram 2

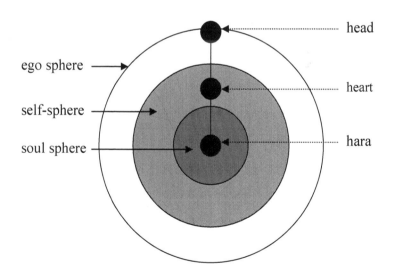

Diagram 3

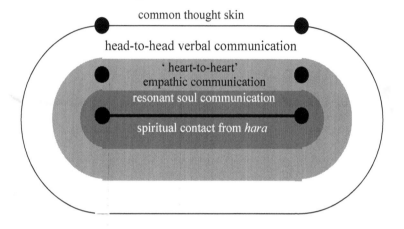

common thought skin

head-to-head verbal communication

' heart-to-heart'
empathic communication

resonant soul communication

spiritual contact from *hara*

Diagram 3 shows the three levels of one-to-one communication that correspond to the mind sphere, body sphere and soul-spiritual sphere respectively.

Head-to-head verbal communication, when successful, creates a common verbal thought skin that contains and unites the mind souls of two individuals.

This containing verbal thought skin may, in turn, facilitate and reflect an empathic 'heart-to-heart' communication uniting the body-souls of two individuals.

Resonant soul communication is an experience of a yet deeper level of communication – an experience of inner soul communion and direct inner contact with another from one's spiritual core in the hara. It is sensed as the creation of a common soul skin and the unification of the soul spheres of two individuals.

What is spiritual seeing and hearing?

We do not see and hear because we have eyes and ears. We have eyes and ears because we are seeing and hearing beings. Spiritually, we see another person not by looking at their body with our eyes but by seeing the human *being* that looks out through their eyes. Similarly, we hear another person not by listening to the sounds their body makes when they speak, but by hearing the being that speaks through sounds. We can see and hear spiritually only by looking and listening, not just with our eyes and ears, but with and from our whole being. As Heidegger put it so simply: *"We* hear, not the ear." When we listen spiritually we are 'all ear', listening with our whole being. This type of hearing is closer to feeling than the hearing of the ears. We feel what we hear. Conversely, we hear what we feel, sensing the expression of *tonalities* of feeling. What we feel and hear are these 'feeling tones' or 'soul tones'. The felt inner resonance of a sound is something *soundless*, consisting of felt tones of silence. Like vocal and musical tones these have different felt qualities – of warmth or coolness, brightness or darkness, lightness or heaviness, sharpness or smoothness etc. That is why musicians and painters speak of tone colours or colour tones. An individual's soul qualities – of warmth or coolness, for example – are also felt tonal qualities, felt qualities of their own underlying soul tones. Some with visual clairvoyance may perceive these soul tones visually as the colours of their 'aura'. They may seek to interpret these colours without, in any way, *feeling* them as the expression of that person's soul – sensing them directly as colourations of that person's own awareness of themselves and the world. This is *not* spiritual seeing. On the other hand, someone may directly feel the basic mood or tonality of another person's awareness of the world and other people – sensing their inner soul tones. This *is* spiritual hearing. It is also the basis of true spiritual seeing. For, the true clairvoyant does not merely 'see' things that others do not. They are *within* the images they behold in their mind's eye, sensing them as the visual expressions of different shapes and colourations of soul, and 'hearing' these spiritually as the expression of underlying soul tones. The relation between spiritual seeing and hearing is like the relation between the visual drama that unfolds on an operatic stage, the arias that are sung and the music played by the orchestra. If we merely 'see' the opera, we see nothing – for we hear nothing. From this point of view even the deaf or blind can 'hear' and 'see' more than the sighted. For they *feel* what they do *not* hear or see, and can use their felt sense to enter into resonance with what others may see or hear but do not *feel*. Spiritual deafness and blindness is far more widespread than physical deafness or blindness. It is also a far more serious 'disability' – a lack of attunement to *feeling tone* and an incapacity to feel an inner soul *resonance* with what they see and hear.

What are our spiritual senses?

Spiritual knowledge is not founded on the use of our five senses alone, but also on a *sixth* and *seventh* sense. The sixth sense is our soul's felt sense of *meaning*. There is an active side of 'meaning' however, and that is the capacity to 'mean'. For as beings, we have the capacity not just to feel and express meanings but to actively *mean* what we do and say. The seventh sense, however, is our capacity not just to mean 'something' but to mean someone. To really mean the words "I love you", for example, is to really mean this *one* 'you' and no other. It is not merely to mean and express 'something' but to mean someone, a being. The difficulty that people have in saying the words "I love you" and meaning them arises because love itself is our capacity to really *mean* another being. This is something we rarely do when we speak to others, focussed as we are on what we are saying, the meaning we are expressing – and not on who we are speaking to – the being we are addressing. To truly address another being we must be able to sense what our words or actions will mean to *them* and not just what they mean to us. Our seventh sense is a spiritual sense – our felt sense of another being, and of what is meaningful to them. Only through a combination of both our sixth and seventh senses can we pass from a felt sense of meaning to a felt resonance with other beings. Everything we say that not only comes from our soul, from our felt sense of *meaning*, but also from a felt sense of another *being* and what is meaningful to that being; everything that is then said in such a way as to truly *mean this being* – everything said in this way says "I love you", for it is the expression of a *felt resonance* with the other.

What is spiritual intimacy?

The twentieth century saw a dramatic lifting of taboos on sexuality and a rise in people's preparedness for emotional openness and intimacy with one another. Yet it has seen no lifting of the taboo on *spiritual* intimacy and intercourse with others. The ordinary understanding is still that we get closer to other people through emotional or physical intimacy, by talking or touching rather than through the sort of wordless inner contact and communication that unites mother and infant, and that lovers experience through the mutual gaze. According to John Heron: "In the strict sense of the term, actual encounter occurs only in mutual touching and mutual gazing, for it is only in these instances that each meets the other meeting him." But the fact that people look at each other does not guarantee that they make resonant inner contact through their mutual gaze. Similarly, the fact that one person touches another person's body does not mean that they touch them in their essential being. Physical contact and intimacy is no guarantee of spiritual contact and intimacy – resonant inner touch. The secret of spiritual touch – resonant inner touch – lies again in *meaning* the other in their essential being – intending to touch them and not just their body. A lover gazing into the eyes of a loved one and placing a hand on theirs, means the other and establishes resonant inner contact. Simply 'laying hands' on another person, even after invoking the holy spirit or cosmic energy, does no more than suggest such genuine inner contact – a contact made from one being to another, as an I to a Thou.

Western culture is a culture in which spiritual intimacy – resonant inner contact – is taboo *except* in the context of intimate family or sexual relationships. The search for intimate *relationships* replaces the capacity for *intimate relating*. Intimacy is identified with emotional sharing or sex. In contrast to Western culture, Japanese culture has preserved, for a long time, a respect for *silence* as a medium of a type of wordless inner contact and communication felt in the belly or *hara*. The medium of this silent 'belly talk' is provided by withholding immediate reactions to another person's words, and instead attending to their inner resonances and allowing these to linger in one's soul. In this way a type of resonant inner communication begins to be experienced that requires no talk at all, but rides on felt tones of silence. This communication can also be experienced as a type of direct umbilical *contact* with the other, issuing instead from the *tanden* – the still-point of silence in the lower abdomen below the navel, the abdomen being literally an 'abode' of the soul. Spiritual knowledge or *gnosis* is a type of intimate inner knowing that transforms both the knower and the known. Really getting to know another being changes and transforms us, revealing not just new dimensions of the other but of our own being too. Gnostic spirituality, as soma-spirituality, is the experience of genuine spiritual intimacy and intercourse with other beings – an intercourse through which we seed and are seeded by the spirit of our own and other people's soul qualities. As a result, we become pregnant with new and hitherto unknown aspects of ourselves – new qualities of soul that we previously identified only with others.

What is spiritual 'growth' or 'development' ?

Spiritual development is not just *self*-development but is about *becoming other* than who we believed we were before. It is about discovering ways of thinking, feeling and relating that were once unknown, alien or foreign to us – or that we may have identified with other people rather than ourselves. A previously foreign way of thinking, feeling and relating can then become part of who we are. That is to say, we no longer treat it as *other-than-self,* but accept it as *another self.* For a time it may feel as if, discovering this other self, we had become a new person. But gradually, we integrate its 'spirit' into our whole self. The process can be compared to adding a new letter to our name, one that, until we are used to it, changes its whole sound even though the old letters are still there. There are times in each of our lives when, through attunement to new aspects of our own spiritual soul, we are aware of approaching our lives in a different 'spirit'. It is not just that we 'have' different feelings, or feel differently 'about' ourselves and about our lives. *We* feel different – our very feeling or sense of self is altered and we are aware of a different spirit within us that we find ourselves able to embody and live out. Similarly, we do not just 'have' different thoughts. We think in and speak in an altogether different way – with a different focus and in a different 'spirit'. At the same time we approach our relationships differently, not necessarily because we move into or out of relationships, but because we ourselves are able to relate in a different way and with a different spirit – to make contact and communicate with others from a different place in our souls.

What are 'spirits' ?

"The relation that constitutes knowing is one in which *we ourselves* are related and in which this relation *vibrates* through our basic posture." Martin Heidegger. What we call 'spirits' are the quintessential qualities of soul that link us, in vibratory resonance, with the beingness or 'quiddity' of things and people. If we are spiritually attuned to nature we resonate with the spirits of wind and sea, sun and rain, animals and plants, rocks and trees, acknowledging. If we are spiritually attuned to a person we resonate with their soul qualities and with the spiritual quintessence of their individuality.

What is your 'spirit' ?

Your spirit is your own larger identity or spiritual self, an identity that includes not only aspects of the self you know, but a vast pool of potentialities latent within your spiritual soul. These potentialities can never be fully expressed and embodied in any one life. Just as our own *actual* abilities in this life can only be fulfilled through a multiplicity of life-roles and relationships, so can our spiritual potentials only be fulfilled through a multiplicity of lives. Spirit, essentially is that which *bodies*. To body our innermost being or spirit, requires many lives, many bodies.

What are spiritual 'values'?

Spiritual values are not 'shared values' but potential ways of *being and relating* that stem from our spiritual soul and are comparable to spiritual genes. Each of these potentials can be experienced as an inner soul quality with its own 'spirit'. Some of these soul qualities we feel as our own, expressing and embodying their spirit in our relationships with others. Others we dis-identify from, identifying them only *with* aspects of other people that we either like or dislike, accept or reject, value or devalue.

What is spiritual health?

Medicine and psychiatry define health only as the normal 'functioning' of mind and body that allows the individual to function economically and generate economic values. Spiritual health is *value fulfilment* – our capacity to fulfil our innermost spiritual values. Spiritual values can be fulfilled by valuing not only those soul qualities we already identify with but by learning to value other soul qualities latent within us – qualities that find their reflection in others. Only by actively *valuing* the *inner soul qualities* of others, irrespective of how they are expressed in their *outer behaviour*, can we enter into resonance with new and hitherto latent aspects or soul qualities of our own. Spiritual health as value fulfilment is an expansion of identity that takes place though a relational process – the *karmic* process. This karmic process is the process of learning to feel, live out and fulfil qualities of soul belonging to our own larger identity or Spirit – in particular those soul qualities which we may have previously devalued or rejected, identifying them with others, or with the particular *way* in which other people express and embody them in their beliefs and behaviour.

What is the spiritual meaning of illness?

When we are unwell, we do not *feel ourselves*. Our bodies or minds feel foreign to us. This sense of foreignness has to do with new aspects of our being which are seeking expression in our everyday life and relationships, but whose essential 'spirit' we have not yet learnt to find a way to fully feel and embody as a *quality of soul*. As a result these spirits haunt and 'possess' us in the form of mental or physical symptoms which medicine then blames on foreign bodies such as viruses or toxins or malign 'spirits'.

What is the relation of health and reincarnation?

The process of spiritual value fulfilment can also be understood as a process of continuous incarnation and re-incarnation within *this* life, involving the birth of new aspects of our inner being and the embodiment of their soul qualities or 'spirits'. Some of these soul qualities may constitute a resonant link with other lives and incarnations. The 're-incarnation' of these qualities is then a healthy expansion of our own spiritual identity in this life. Reincarnation, in this sense, is not the karmic 'cause' of illness but its cure. The healing process of re-incarnation or re-embodiment can be compared to the process an actor goes through in learning to incarnate or embody the 'spirit' of a new part. Each part the actor plays brings out a face or facet of their own being, a new way of looking out on the world and relating to others. Illness can be compared to the dis-ease of an actor who is uneasy with a new part, or a musician uneasy with a new piece – unable or unwilling to resonate with its spirit and personify that spirit in performance.

What is spirit healing?

We may or may not allow ourselves to breath in the spirits that hang in the atmosphere around us, emanated by the things and people in our environment. We may or may not allow ourselves to fully acknowledge or embody the spirits that circulate within our resonant soul. Instead we may experience them only indirectly, as bodily sensations and mental thoughts. Spirit healing is not 'spiritualistic' healing – the invocation of a universal *Spirit* or life energy to cure disease. Nor is it spiritistic healing, the attempt to cure disease by banishing malign *spirits*. Spirit healing is not about *banishing* but about *bodying* the spirits within us, allowing them to permeate our body-soul and mind soul, recognising them as meaningful qualities of soul and allowing them to find expression in our bodily moods and demeanour. That is why people recovering from a serious illness so often find themselves changed, not the same as they were before, imbued with a new 'spirit' that they feel able to fully embody and express. It is only those spirits that we refrain from fully bodying, that we feel as foreign or not-self, that we fear or view as evil – that then nevertheless haunt our bodies or minds. They may haunt us as spectres we perceive around us with our sentient soul. They may haunt our mind soul as mental spirits such as voices heard in our heads. Or they may haunt our body-soul as body spirits. An individual's body-soul bears within it the somatic trace or imprint of everybody they have known in this life and in others – not least those who have persecuted, abused or violated them in some way. Were these body spirits not present we could not dream the bodies of others. But body spirits that we cannot consciously attune to in our own resonant soul may become trapped in our body-soul and find expression as body nightmares – disturbing somatic sensations or symptoms. The dis-ease occasioned by these body spirits may finally express itself in somatic disorders. Healing our minds and bodies is also not simply a matter of blaming illness on foreign bodies, such as micro-organisms or cancerous cells, and banishing it with modern witchdoctery – the use of medical or psychiatric drugs. It can only come about through *resonance* with body spirits. For it is through such resonance that they are released from entrapment in our mind- and body-souls, and can circulate freely in our resonant souls. Only in this way can they be mentally and emotionally neutralised, felt not as malign spirits but pure tones and textures of feeling that can simply blend into the rich music of our spiritual souls.

What is spiritual 'karma' ?

The true meaning of 'karma' has nothing to do with reward and punishment, with receiving blessings for good deeds performed in the past or being punished for our past-life sins. Meaning itself has to do with *change*. Karma is a meaningful process of change or metamorphosis that belongs to the very essence of life. It is not about what you *do* or have *done* but about who you are – your inner *being*. The karmic process is the process of learning to become who you are by *becoming other* – finding another deeper self within you and rediscovering your own other selves. We can discover different aspects of our own inner being by learning to resonate with the essential spirit or differing soul qualities of *others* – other individuals and groups, races and religions, cultures and nations. *Positive karma* is the capacity to grow and change by resonating with the soul qualities of others and thereby get to know new aspects of ourselves. *Negative karma* is accrued by dis-identifying from latent soul qualities of our own and instead identifying them only with others. It is these disowned soul qualities that return to haunt us. Positive and negative karma however, go hand in hand. No one can fully identify, let alone identify *with*, all the aspects of their inner being, all the spirits that lie latent in their spiritual soul. Negative karma helps us *identify* these aspects by first of all feeling and confronting them as *something other-than-self*. By then attuning to the *spirits* of these aspects, we can transform this negative karma into positive karma – resonating and identifying with them as dimensions of our own larger spiritual identity.

What is the soma-psychology of birth and infancy?

The body-soul of the mother is the womb of her child's body-soul, and the spirit that will ensoul it from within. Within the womb and even after birth the baby spends much of the time 'asleep' – that is to say, *awake* in its own spiritual body and spiritual soul. The baby has a body-soul and a sentient soul but no resonant soul or mind soul of its own. After birth, the infant continues to dwell in the womb of its own body-soul or *soma-psyche* – still intimately linked with that of the mother. To begin with it continues to develop its sensory skin and to expand its sentient soul. Only gradually does it begin to develop an ego skin and self skin. Only much later, if at all, will it learn to feel its *soul skin* as the inner surface of its own resonant soul.
  If the mother lacks contact with her own resonant soul she cannot attune to that of the infant, and help it to embody and express it. If her face is a fixed mask of her soul she cannot help the infant to become a person – to literally personify its own soul by allowing inner tones of feeling to *sound through* its voice (*per-sonare*) and find full expression in its face and eyes. If she is out of touch with her own spiritual core she cannot make real inner contact with the infant – addressing and touching it as a *being* – no matter how gently or roughly she speaks to it or handles its body. If an infant or child is treated as an object or "It" rather than as an embodied being or "Thou" it will grow up lacking a strong bodily sense of self and a felt bodily awareness of its own individual soul and spirit. Its body and mind may develop normally, but its soul and spirit will not – since, for this, it needs the nourishment of soul-spiritual contact with other

beings. However healthy its body and 'normal' its mind, the adult will experience a sense of soul-spiritual deadness and a deep sense of emptiness that comes from inner contact starvation – a deprivation of spiritual contact and soul resonance with others no amount of social contact or emotional 'empathy' will make up for.

What we think of in the West as 'normal' or 'healthy' child development is in fact something quite abnormal and unhealthy, restricting both the child's and the adult's awareness to their own body-soul and mind soul. The resonant soul is sealed off by an armouring self skin – a reactive emotional surface – and by a defensive ego skin. The child's ego skin develops through language acquisition, but language is acquired in such a way that few children or adults ever find their own authentic voice. To do so, they need to sense language itself as a 'second skin' echoing their own resonant soul. But words are learnt merely as names for concrete things or abstract concepts, and the child never experiences their wordless inner sense or resonance. We dwell within the world as we dwell within the word. If we cannot feel inner dimensions of meaning within the word we cannot feel inner dimensions of meaning in the world itself. As a result, we cannot experience our outer world *as* word, as something that addresses us in our souls and calls forth a resonant inner response from them.

The *self-skin* of the child is rigidified by actively discouraging them from *embodying* their inner soul responses – revealing their inner soul moods in their outer body language. Most adults end up with a 'body language' whose alphabet and vocabulary of looks and facial expression, vocal tones and amplitudes, postures and gestures is so poor that it cannot possibly give expression to the rich inner language of their resonant souls – the *music* of feeling tone. A restricted and rigidified outer body language restricts the individual's inner bodily self-awareness and bodily sense of self. It also restricts the natural mobility and expressiveness of their inner body as such – their body of soul and spirit. *Spirit* and *soul* require *soma* if the human mind and body are not to become their prison. Emotional literacy is not enough without the capacity to embody feelings.

Every feeling is an embodiment attuned in this or that way, a mood that embodies in this or that way. Heidegger

Every step in spiritual development, as Buddhist tradition recognises, brings with it a new sense of our own bodies. Indeed it creates an entirely new body, for it is the *embodiment* of a new and deeper mode of being and relating, one that can only come from resonance with new and deeper moods of soul. Truly spiritual modes of being and relating are realised through soma-spirituality – the embodiment of deeply spiritual moods of soul. These moods belong to our spiritual soul, a soul we have access to only through our resonant soul. The abode of this soul is the abdominal womb of our bodily soul – the hara. The path to soma-spirituality leads from head and heart, mind soul and body-soul, to *hara awareness*.

HARA AWARENESS
ELEMENTARY EXERCISES

It must be emphasised from the outset that *head, heart and hara* are not 'energy centres' or 'chakra' but centres of *awareness*. Awareness has both a focus and a locus. We may be conscious of the focus of our awareness, but we are less conscious of its centre or locus. Yoga meditation is about becoming aware of, or focussing our awareness on, different energy centres. But from what centre or locus of awareness do we do so? Hara meditation, on the other hand, is not about focussing our awareness on different centres but about moving the locus of our awareness between those centres. In particular, it is the capacity to move the locus or 'coordinate point' of our awareness from our head and/or heart centre to our hara or abdominal centre. There is an inherent paradox, however, in talking of centres or loci of awareness. The paradox lies in the fact that such centres are *points* in an inner space of awareness - points we can only become aware of by looking into that space from its periphery. The 'light' of awareness radiates outwards from different *points* or centres of awareness within us. Awareness, however, is also something that radiates inward from our periphery towards those centres. To learn to look into ourselves we must first learn to identify with the surface bodily periphery of our awareness and open up inner spaces of awareness within different regions of our bodies. It is only from this surface bodily periphery of our awareness that we can look into those inner spaces of awareness, identify different points or centres of awareness within them, and thus learn to look out from those different centres. The soul-body is a peripheral sphere or 'psychic envelope' *of* awareness with both an outer and inner surface. Through its outer surface, as through the pores of our skin, we quite literally absorb and breathe in our awareness of the world around us. From its inner surface we look into a soul-space of awareness with its three main centres. From each of the centres we have a qualitatively different experience of space as such. Locating our awareness at different centres, we quite literally enter a *qualitatively* different space and experience both our inner soul-space and the outer world-space in a qualitatively different way.

Looking out at the world from the head centre *alone* we experience ourselves as self-enclosed subjects reflecting its light. From our chest region and heart centre we can experience our own awareness as something with its own intrinsic qualities of *airiness, light and radiance*, a light that we can allow to brighten and radiate through our eyes. The chest surface of our *soul-body* is an open porous surface through which we breathe in our awareness of the world around us – absorbing the light that streams into us in a way that draws the light of awareness from our heart centre and allows this light not only to radiate from our eyes but to emanate from our entire upper body surface, head and chest. Unlike head and heart, however, the *hara* is not one centre among others from which our awareness itself *radiates outward* as soul light. Instead it is *the* centre towards which our awareness *radiates inward* as *inner soul darkness* – and at the same time fills our bellies with *inner soul warmth*. As awareness rises from the *hara* towards heart and head, this dark, fluid soul warmth becomes transformed, first into the element of 'air' or soul-breath, then into an element of soul-light infusing that air. The combination of light and air is the dry 'life-fire' or lightning of the soul. The combination of fluidity and air forms the emotional moisture that rises to form clouds of awareness, ready to descend as emotional rain. As our awareness radiates inward towards its centre of awareness in the hara – known in Japanese as the *tanden* - it reaches no end. The *tanden* is a 'point at infinity' or 'inward infinitude' that can lead us ever further *down into* ourselves, into our own *unbounded interiority* of the psyche. This is the "dark sea of awareness" (Castaneda). It is through the *inwardly unbounded depths and breadths* of this 'sea of awareness' that we connect to the *withinness* of everything and everyone *around* us. The philosophy of hara is a reminder of a basic spiritual truth: that it is only by moving down into *ourselves* and towards our innermost centre that we can make genuine *inner* contact with other people, and feel a genuine *inner* connectedness with the cosmos.

SENSING YOUR THREE SOUL CENTRES

1. Close your eyes or simply withdraw the *focus* of your gaze to a point just in front of and between your eyes. Doing so, become fully aware of your head and the surface of your face. Now feel the top, sides and back of your head. Feel your whole head as if it were a hollow vessel with its own inner space. Sense a centre or *locus* of awareness in this space, just between your eyes and behind your forehead. As you inhale air through your nose, feel the inner space of your head filling with awareness. As it does so allow your eyes to open (wider). Feel your awareness coming fully into your eyes and fully upfront to the surface of your face. Allow the focus of your gaze to reach forward again into the space in front of you, and feel yourself looking out at the world from the centre or locus of awareness in your head

2. With you eyes closed, bring your awareness down into the region of your chest. Feel the front surface of your chest, the surface of your back, the sides of your ribcage. Feel your ribcage and chest as a whole, as a hollow vessel. Breathe entirely with your chest muscles and feel the rise and fall of your breast as you inhale and exhale. In your own time gradually open your eyes, stay aware of the surface of your chest and at the same time become aware of the surfaces of the objects and walls around you. Feel yourself absorbing your awareness of these surfaces through the surface of your chest. As you breathe in, sense your chest expanding and filling not only with air but with light – the light of your awareness of the space around you. Sense a centre of awareness in the region of your heart from which the light of your own awareness is drawn out.

3. Close your eyes and become aware of your entire lower body below the waist. Feel your legs and the contact of your feet with the ground. Now bring your awareness fully into your abdomen. Feel a warm dark space of awareness opening up within your abdomen and feel yourself breathing into that space rather than into the inner space of your chest. Feel the surface of your abdomen swell and expand like a balloon as you breathe in, and sense it filling with a dark, fluid warmth as you do so. Sense a centre of awareness a few inches below and behind the navel. In your own time, half open your eyes, keeping your lids low. Feel yourself looking out from the centre of awareness in your abdomen. Now focus on an object in the space in front of you, and feel yourself inwardly connected to its own *withinness* from the centre of awareness within your abdomen and through its own aware withinness.

HARA MEDITATION AND HARA BREATHING

Hara meditation is all about centring our awareness in the abdomen. Hara breathing is all about breathing from and with the abdomen. Because the hara is our spiritual and physical centre of gravity we can do neither unless we are able to balance our normal upper body awareness with lower body awareness. To do so we must first learn to shift our awareness entirely from our upper body to our lower body, below the waist. The upper body regions, head and chest, are where we experience all the motion and commotion of our mental and emotional life. At any time we can remove ourselves from this commotion, simply by shifting our awareness entirely to our lower body or underbody. To do so you can simply imagine that you are standing or sitting in a calm lake or sea that reaches up to your waist – a lake or sea of inner silence.

Hara Meditation

1. Feel your *upper body* as a whole, head and chest, and sense its substantiality.
2. Shift your awareness to your entire *lower body*, feeling its substantiality and the contact of your feet with the ground.
3. Focus on your abdomen or *hara*, and feel it as a dark, warm, womblike abode in which you can come to rest and abide within yourself.
4. Sense a still-point of silence in the inner space of your abdomen, a few inches below and behind the navel, and sense yourself listen into this still-point of silence.

Hara Breathing

1. With your mouth firmly closed, breathe entirely from your abdomen, feeling it gently push out and expand as you inhale, and gently drawing it in as you exhale. Never suck air in through your nose by expanding your chest.
2. Whenever you exhale, allow your breath to slow down and come to a halt for some time, gently pressing it down into the abdomen, before beginning to slowly and imperceptibly draw breath in again from your abdomen.
3. Even as your out-breath of air slows to a halt, feel a *continuing* out-breath of awareness flowing down from your abdomen to the very ground beneath you.
4. With each out-breath feel this flow of awareness descending ever deeper below this ground – as if entering and spreading out into a deep dark, underground sea of awareness.

Normally we think of and experience our breathing as a singular cycle of in-and out-breath (see Diagram 1). Little are we aware that the lower turning point of this cycle, the 'zero-point' where out-breath gives way to in-breath, leads into a second, deeper dimension of the breath cycle (Diagram 2). The essence of hara breathing is not merely to mechanically slow down and 'hold' our breath as we reach this point, but to experience our exhalation continuing as an out-breath of awareness. Truly 'deep' breathing, in other words, has nothing do to with aerobics. It belongs to the lower part of the breath cycle which is entirely *anaerobic* in nature, a cycle in which we inhale and exhale the 'life-breath' of awareness itself – that which the Greeks called *psyche*.

Diagram 1 - the singular breath cycle

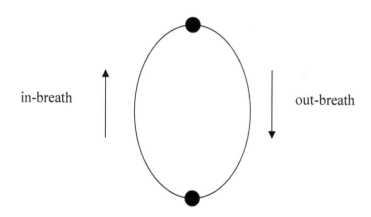

in-breath   out-breath

Diagram 2 - the double breath cycle

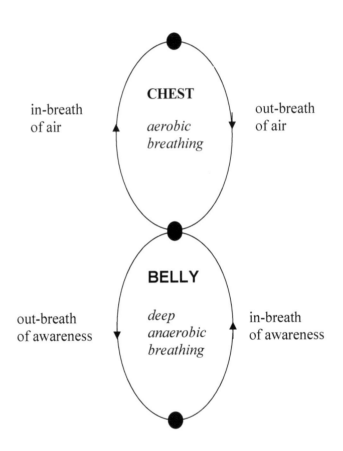

'Hara breathing' and 'hara meditation' are united through this double cycle in which we experience the metamorphosis or transubstantiation of bodily breathing into a deep meditative awareness through the central turning point of the double breath cycle. It is at this point at which our *awareness of breathing*, normally centred in our chest and above the diaphragm, transforms into a *breathing of awareness* centred in our lower belly or abdomen.

The dotted line in Diagram 3 that cuts across the central turning point of the double breath cycle is what I term the *diaphragm of awareness*, a threshold of both breath and awareness just below the waist. Both our breath and awareness need to be pressed and held down below this threshold. Only in this way can our awareness move fully down the line of descent – a line that takes us from our head centre or *outer ego*, through our heart and hara centre – the tanden – right down into the bottomless *inner ground* of our being.

Diagram 3

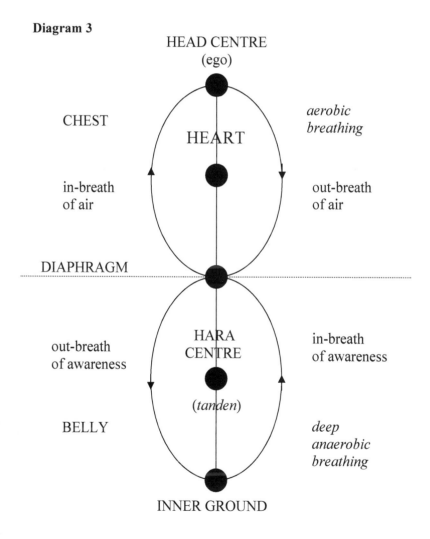

HEAD CENTRE
(ego)

CHEST

HEART

aerobic breathing

in-breath
of air

out-breath
of air

DIAPHRAGM

HARA
CENTRE

out-breath
of awareness

in-breath
of awareness

(*tanden*)

BELLY

deep anaerobic breathing

INNER GROUND

What people experience today as 'depression' is only possible in a culture in which people have lost the capacity to actively press down or *de-press* their breathing and awareness below the diaphragm. Having lost hara awareness they feel dis-located from the true centre and inner ground of their being. As a result they experience this centre and that ground as something negative that *pulls them down* towards a black hole through which they dare not pass, into dark depths of their being to which they dare not descend. For those *with* hara awareness, on the other hand, ordinary feelings of dejection or deprivation, dis-ease or distress, disappointment or disillusionment are all experienced not as a state of depression to be suffered but as spurs to an active meditative *de-pression* of awareness - one that helps us to *dis-illusion* our egos, disidentify from our heads and hearts, and re-identify with our deeper selves and reground ourselves in the innermost depths of our being.

HARA TOUCH – the experience of inner contact and connectedness

The fact that someone touches a part of your body does not guarantee that you will feel touched in your being. The fact that they look at your eyes does not mean that they really look at and see you – touching the very core of your being through their gaze. The significance of the hara is recognised in many Oriental touch therapies such as Reiki or Shiatsu. But touching some part of another person's body – even their belly or abdomen – is not the same as touching *them* from the core of our being, and touching the core of their being. We can be touched by someone's words or gaze without physical contact. Making inner contact with others is not about touching their bodies, but touching them as beings – and doing so from the very depths and core of our being. To do so we must first contact those depths and that core through our own centre of awareness in our hara.

What follows is a pair exercise which offers the experience of making deep 'umbilical' contact with others from the hara centre or tanden – touching them inwardly from your centre of awareness in the lower belly or abdomen, or feeling inwardly touched by a partner as they make inner contact with you from their hara. To begin with, arrange two chairs or stools so that you sit close up and face to face with your partner. Make sure that your eyes are roughly level, your backs straight and the chairs or stools on which you are seated high enough so that your upper legs are horizontal and at right angles to your lower legs. Place your hands on your thighs or knees. Then take it in turns to give each other the following instructions:

1. Look at my eyes and place one of your hands on mine.

2. (...pause) Take your hand away again.

3. Now close your eyes and bring your awareness fully into your lower body, feeling the contact of your feet with the ground. Centre both your breathing and your awareness in your lower belly, and feel a centre of awareness there, a couple of inches below and behind the navel.

4. (...pause) In your own time begin to open your eyes and look at mine again, but this time with the intent to really see me and not just my eyes, connecting with m   e not just through your eyes but umbilically – from a centre of awareness in your hara to a centre of awareness in mine.

5. As you begin to feel this inner contact, place your hand on mine again, but this time with the intent to really touch me and not just my hand. Allow the pressure of your hand on mine to reflect the degree of inner umbilical contact you feel you are making with me.

6. Now in your own time, remove your hand and still feel umbilically in touch with me from the centre of awareness in your hara.

7. Now in your own time, gradually avert your gaze, whilst feeling in touch with your self through your centre of awareness in the hara.

HARA VOICE – insounding and intoning from the hara

1. With your mouth closed, hear yourself say the word 'hara' in your head. Do this several times, noticing the pitch of your inner voice as you hear it in your head. Now silently mouth the word 'hara' as if you were speaking it with a 'head voice' without breath and resonance in the inner space of your chest.
2. With your mouth closed, hear yourself say the word 'hara', but this time feel as if the word was being inwardly uttered from the region of your heart, and at a significantly lower pitch. Now silently mouth the word 'hara', feeling your breath and inner voice coming from your chest.
3. Hear yourself inwardly utter the word 'hara' *from* your hara, doing so with an inner voice with the deepest possible bass tone - one that comes from the depths of your belly and the depths of your being. Now very slowly mouth the word 'hara' with your mouth wide open, and with a deep inner tone of voice and a deep inner flow of breath that comes entirely from your abdomen.

Without hara voice we cannot experience and embody our 'fundamental tone', the tone that we strike within ourselves when head and hara are united like nodes of a single-stringed instrument or monochord. If the *higher harmonics* of this fundamental tone are sounded without it (like plucking an instrument) an individual's voice, no matter how deep in tone, lacks inner resonance.

HARA DIAGNOSIS

Outward hara diagnosis is about feeling or 'palpating' different regions of another person's belly and abdomen, each of which is thought to correspond to different organs of the body. *Inner* hara diagnosis is quite different. It is about using one's own felt body to feel another person's body from within – sensing the inner shape, tone and coordinate points of awareness of their own felt body. The soul is the felt *inwardness* of the body. The body is the perceived *outwardness* of the soul. Sensing another person's inwardly felt body with your own is akin to experiencing their soul in your body or your soul in their body.

1. Look at a person and feel the basic inner mood or tonality of awareness that their *bodies* are emanating at that point in time.

2. Now take a *mental snapshot* of their outer posture, facial expression and the look in their eyes and then immediately turn away.

3. With your eyes still open, hold this mental image of the other person's body in your *mind's eye*, sensing the facial expression and look in their eyes as if it were yours.

4. At the same time continue to sense in your own *body* the basic mood or tonality of awareness they emanated.

5. *Resonate back and forth* between your inner *bodily sense* of the other person and the outer picture you have of them in your *mind's eye* until you feel fully in resonance with the other – sensing their soul in your body, face and eyes.

6. Sense *where and how* you feel the soul of the other in your body, and in this way feel the shape, tone and texture of their own inwardly felt body. Sense where their bodily self-awareness is concentrated or centred, the intensity of their upper and lower body awareness, and the relation, or lack of it, between their head, heart and hara centres.

7. Sense also the *overall spatiality* of the other person's felt body – whether and to what degree their gaze is turned inwards towards their core or radiates outward from their eyes and body surface, whether and to what degree their awareness is 'spaced out' or 'spaced in', whether and to what degree their bodily periphery feels bounded and closed off or receptive and open.

Repeat the exercise frequently at other times, with the same person or other people.

HEALING FROM HARA

Hara diagnosis allows one to sense not only the main locus or coordinate point of another person's body of awareness, but the relationship between their three main centres of awareness and their capacity to centre and ground their awareness in their hara. Also, by bringing one's own soul-body into resonance with that of another person, and allowing it to shift shape in resonance with its different centres, tones and textures, hara diagnosis offers the opportunity for hara healing – helping others to centre and ground their awareness in their hara. One does so by gradually and imperceptibly modulating the basic tone and texture of one's own soul-body from a state of initial *resonance* with the felt body of the other to a state of centeredness, groundedness and 'health' or *soundness*. This is a state in which the head, heart and hara centres of our organism, like nodes of a single-stringed instrument or monochord, give expression to the 'fundamental tone' of our inner organism or soul-body. Understood as a musical instrument or *organon,* our soul organism is constantly resounding in and through our bodies, its inner tones and chords finding expression in nerve and muscle tone, the tone of our words and deeds, voice and body language. Healing from hara can be compared to a spontaneous vocal or musical dialogue in which we not only hearken to the *undertones* of another person's voice tones or musical notes, words or body language, bringing ourselves into resonance with them, but use our own inner voice to modulate the undertone of our response – communicating wordlessly through our voice and body language in a way which subtly transforms the basic tone of another person's inner bodily self-awareness.

Hara healing follows a threefold cycle of *receptivity, resonance* and *response*:

1. *Outer receptivity* to another person's words and body language.
2. *Inner resonance* with the inner bodily feeling tones it communicates.
3. Using our own words and body language to *respond outwardly* in a way that communicates a deepening *inner* attunement to our own 'fundamental tone'.

The three main mediums of hara healing are: resonant listening, resonant touch and resonant eye-contact.

Example exercise: resonant eye-contact

Adopt the face to face position for HARA TOUCH and make eye-contact with your partner. Then:

1. Become *receptive* to the gaze of the other and attune to a particular emotional quality or 'tonality' of their gaze.

2. Bring your whole felt body into *resonance* with this particular quality of feeling tone, and reflect it back to your partner through the tone of your own gaze.

3. *Respond* through a subtle modulation of your gaze which gradually begins to radiate a new quality of feeling tone more grounded in your 'fundamental tone'.

EXPANDING A COSMIC SPHERE OF AWARENESS

1. Become aware of the spaces around your body – the spaces that reach out on either side of you, in front of you and behind you, above your head and below your feet.

2. Feel your entire body surface front and back, as an open and porous surface, breathing in your awareness of the entire space around you.

3. Sense your hara centre as the central *point* of a vast cosmic space of awareness surrounding your body.

4. Feel your body surface drawing in an *invisible light of awareness* from the periphery of this space, a light which radiates inwardly from this periphery.

5. Feel this all-round, inwardly streaming light permeating the surface of your own body and making its periphery feel more open and porous.

6. Sense this light expanding the spaces between the atoms and molecules of your body as it radiates inwardly towards your hara centre.

7. Feel your body becoming more and more spacious, light and diffuse, as if expanding into cosmic space, whilst at the same time feeling ever more centred in your hara.

THE LANGUAGE OF 'HARA'
Traditional Japanese Terms and Idioms

Hara-gei
'belly play/belly art' - the art of wordless, subliminal communication issuing directly from the hara.

Hara o saguru
A person deeply probing another 'feels around with his hara'.
The art of *handling* others directly with the hara rather than via the hands themselves

Hara no aru hito
'man with belly' - seated and centred in the hara

Hara no hiroi /semai hito
man with broad/narrow belly - character dispositions

Hara no chiisai hito
'the man with the little belly' - immature

Hara no dekita hito
'man who has finished his belly' - mature human being fit to lead others

Haratsuzumi
'belly drum' - taut and firm abdomen

Hara-goe
'belly voice' - voice of the mature human being, centred in the hara

Hara de Kangaeru
'belly thinking' - to think abdominally, rather than with the head

Hara no nai hito wa, hara de kangaeru ga dekinai
'a man without belly cannot do belly thinking'

Atama de kangaeru
Term of abuse - a man who thinks with his head

148

Hara ga suwatte iru
a person whose belly is sedate, whose hara 'sits'

Hara ga suwatte imasu
the 'seat' of the hara, its low abdominal centre

Hara wo sueru
to 'seat' the hara or 'let it sit'

Hara wo neru
to 'train the belly' - learning to let it sit

Hara si sueru
the result of hara training - learning to bear unpleasant things by letting them come to rest and 'seat themselves in the belly'

Hara ga-tatsu
when someone is angry their hara 'rises' or 'stands up'

Haraise
medical: 'to still the hara'. Behavioural: a fit of rage by someone with an untrained hara that attempts 'to still the hara' by letting it rise

Hara no naka wo watte misemasu
to show what is inside one's belly by opening it - to speak truthfully and sincerely

Hara o waru
a person having a frank talk with another 'cuts his hara open'

Harakiri (common) / **Seppuku** (Samurai)
a fatal incision of the sword made in the region of the hara

Seiza
the practice of sitting and breathing in a way that seats the hara

Koshi / Kyushi
the whole of the trunk / body-soul below the navel

Tanden
bodily site of the hara, about two inches below the level of the navel

BIBLIOGRAPHY

Anzieu, Didier *Psychic Envelopes* Karnac 1990

Aron and Anderson (ed.) *Relational Perspectives on the Body* Analytic Press 1998

Barfield, Owen *Speaker's Meaning* Rudolf Steiner Press 1970

Buber, Martin *I and Thou* T&T Clark 1996

Buber, Martin *On Intersubjectivity and Cultural Creativity* University of Chicago Press 1992

Chiozza, Luis *Hidden Affects in Somatic Disorders* Psychosocial Press 1998

Cupitt, Don *The Religion of Being* SCM Press 1998

Davidson, John *Subtle Energy* C.W.Daniel 1987

Davidson, John *The Secret of the Creative Vacuum* C.W.Daniel 1989

Dürckheim, Karlfried *Hara, The Vital Centre of Man* Unwin 1980

Fiumara *The Metaphoric Process* Routledge 1995

Foucault, Michel *The Birth of the Clinic* Routledge 1989

Fox, Mathew *Meditations with Meister Eckhart* Bear and Company 1983

Gendlin, Eugene *Focusing* Bantam 1979

Gendlin, Eugene *Experiencing and the Creation of Meaning* Northwestern University Press 1997

Gendlin, Eugene *Focusing-oriented Psychotherapy* Guilford Press 1996

Goldstein, Kurt / Sacks, Oliver *TheOrganism* Urzone 1995

Gordon, Paul *Face to Face; Therapy as Ethics* Constable and Compay Ltd. 1999

Heidegger, Martin *Basic Questions of Philosophy* Indiana University Press 1994

Heidegger, Martin *The Fundamental Concepts of Metaphysics* Indiana 1995

Heidegger, Martin *The Principle of Reason* Indiana University Press 1996

Heidegger, Martin *Zollikoner Seminare* Klostermann 1994

Jonas, Hans *The Gnostic Religion* Routledge 1992

Kahn, Charles H. *The Art and Though of Heraclitus* Cambridge 1987

Kuriyama, S. *The Expressiveness of the Body and the Divergence of Greek and Chinese Medicine*
Zone Books 1999

Lakoff and Johnson *Metaphors We Live By* University of Chicago Press 1980

Lewontin, R.C. *Biology as Ideology, the doctrine of DNA* Harper 1993

Levin, David Michael *The Body's Recollection of Being* Routledge 1985

Levin, David Michael *The Listening Self* Routledge 1989

Lewontin, R.C. *Biology as Ideology, the doctrine of DNA* Harper 1993

Maitland, Jeffrey *Spacious Body* North Atlantic Books 1995
Maslow *Towards a Psychology of Being* John Wiley and Sons 1968
Mindell *Working with the Dreaming Body* Arkana 1989
Pagels, Elaine *The Gnostic Gospels* Penguin 1982
Roberts, Jane *Adventures in Consciousness* Moment Point Press 1999
Roberts, Jane *Seth Speaks - The Eternal Validity of the Soul* New World Library 1994
Sheldrake, Rupert *A New Science of Life, The Hypothesis of Morphic Resonance* Park Street Press 1995
Steiner, Rudolf *Metamorphoses of the Soul (2)* Rudolf Steiner Press 1983
Steiner, Rudolf *Mystery of the Universe* Anthroposophic Press 2001
Steiner, Rudolf *Occult Reading and Occult Hearing* Rudolf Steiner Press 1975
Steiner, Rudolf *The Fourth Dimension* Anthroposophic Press 2001
Steiner, Rudolf *The Inner Nature of Music and the Experience of Tone* Anthroposophic Press 1983
Wilberg, Peter *From Psycho-somatics to Soma-semiotics* New Gnosis Publications 2003
Wilberg, Peter *The Qualia Revolution* New Gnosis Publications 2003
Wilberg, Peter *The Therapist as Listener* New Gnosis Publications 2003
Wilberg, P. (1996) *Heidegger and Hara* Journal of the Society for Existential Analysis Vol.8/1
Wilberg, Peter *Listening as Bodywork* Energy and Character 30/2
Wilberg, Peter *Organismic Ontology and Organismic Healing* Energy and Character 31/1
Wilberg, Peter *The Language of Listening*, Journal of the Society for Existential Analysis 3
Wilberg, Peter *Introduction to Maieutic Listening* JSEA 8.1
Winnicott, Donald *The Maturational Process and the Facilitating Environment* Hogarth 1965

10492282R0

Made in the USA
Lexington, KY
15 August 2011